"Michele Howe has a wonderful way of writing so that readers feel her heart in every paragraph. In using her own experiences, Michele helps readers feel she understands and cares about what they are going through. Her book, *Caring for Our Aging Parents*, not only connects with anyone caring for a loved one; it also uses her faith and gives readers practical tools of how to do this well."

—Robyn Besemann
Author and host of *Chained No More* Talk Radio
www.robynbministries.com

"As a former caregiver, I find Michele's caring tips to be spot on. *Caring for Our Aging Parents* offers hope and encouragement for scenarios any caregiver can experience. Her invitation to step momentarily into the lives of other caregivers, to feel their emotions and identify with their concerns, affirms we're not alone. If you're new to caregiving or it's become your way of life, *Caring for Our Aging Parents* will help you in your journey."

—Linda Goldfarb
International author/speaker, Christian life coach
Personality profiler and founder of Parenting Awesome Kids

"Eminently practical yet also keenly inspirational, Michele Howe's *Caring for Our Aging Parents* is the kind of book you don't *want* to need, yet the one you'll be thrilled to own when the time comes to care for a loved one. Packed with personal insights and spiritual fuel for the journey, this book provides the perfect companionship to help transform a challenging phase of life into a gifted opportunity to serve with love."

—Lisa M. Hendey
Author of *The Grace of Yes* and founder of CatholicMom.com

"Caregiving can feel lonely and confusing sometimes. The stories Michele Howe gathered here reveal a range of struggles so that within a few chapters, readers will find others facing similar challenges. These are a gift—a reminder you aren't alone."

—Ann Kroeker
Author of *The Contemplative Mom* and *Not So Fast*
Coauthor of *On Being a Writer*

"Michele Howe has written a compelling new book addressing the challenge many Baby Boomers are now faced with—caring for aging parents. Written with grace and dignity, she powerfully captures the trials faced by people who choose to be caregivers to their elderly parents. Using real-life stories that are both sweet and poignant, she perfectly depicts what we all feel but seldom talk about in these situations. If you have aging parents, you need to read this book!"

—Rick Johnson
Best-selling author of *Overcoming Toxic Parenting*,
10 Things Great Dads Do*, and *Becoming Your Spouse's Better Half

"In *Caring for Our Aging Parents*, the reader gets little glimpses of the myriad challenges (and joys) of looking after loved ones in their last days . . . or years. I've been down this path and, in fact, am a frequent flyer. As Howe explains, 'The irony in caregiving is that to do it well, we need practice. Lots and lots of practice.' I learned so much and continue to glean insight from my mom's last six months on earth eleven years ago. I'm currently tiptoeing through a whole new round of this journey with my 80-something in-laws. I have found the stories Howe shares to be completely relatable, and I keep thinking, 'That's *me*!' Her insight is based on experience, and it shows. Throughout the book, you will be reminded of the necessity of balance . . . compassion and boundaries, caring for them and self-care, your limited love and God's infinite mercy. This book needs to be in the hands of everyone who is or will soon be the go-to caretaker of an aging loved one."

—Diane Markins
Author of *Contentment Connection:*
75 Ways to Grow Joy & Satisfaction

"Writing for women and the seasons of our lives, Michele Howe provides in *Caring for Our Aging Parents* peace and assurance for those transitioning into caretakers for aging family. Whether your relationship with your parent has been comfortable or challenging, Michele gently and skillfully shows us how to draw close and hear God's grace-filled guidance while supporting our aging adults in their sunset years."

—PeggySue Wells
Author of 24 books including *Slavery in the Land of the Free*
Producer and cohost of WBCL's *Mid-Morning*

"In *Caring for Our Aging Parents*, Michele Howe beautifully weaves real-life stories, Scripture, take-away thoughts, and prayers into bite-sized chapters that will encourage any reader facing the challenges of parent care. In these pages, you'll hear the kind voice of a friend who has been there; one who has experienced the difficult questions and emotions that often accompany the role of caregiver. This book is not only a practical resource but also an oasis of refreshing for people who may be feeling stretched by the needs of an elderly parent. I love the devotional style that makes the themes easy to take to heart and makes the lessons readily applicable to one's own unique situation."

—Rachel Anne Ridge
Author of *Flash the Homeless Donkey Who*
Taught Me about Life, Faith, and Second Chances
and *Made to Belong: A Six-Week Journey to Discover Your Purpose*

"Caregiving must be one of the most difficult jobs anyone can undertake. In Michele Howe's *Caring for Our Aging Parents*, you may see yourself. She shares story after story of real-life and complex situations covering a variety of circumstances. She gently weaves her gems of discernment with great depth into the close of each chapter. Her perfect 'heart's cry' prayers are worded to express the desires of caregivers of every type. If you are a caregiver . . . you will realize you are not alone on this often painful path. Michele's encouragement brings renewed faith, insight, and courage for the road ahead."

—Gail Cawley Showalter
Founder, SMORE for Women

"The world is a better place because of the tireless, yet often unappreciated selflessness of caregivers. Michele Howe understands firsthand the challenges, loneliness, and invisibility of that calling. In her book, she comes alongside other caregivers with stories, wisdom, and affirmation to recharge any caregiver's spirits and refuel them for the long journey ahead."

— Carolyn Custis James, author of *Half the Church:*
Recapturing God's Global Vision for Women* and *Malestrom:
Manhood Swept into the Currents of a Changing World

MICHELE HOWE

Caring

— FOR OUR —

Aging Parents

*Lessons in Love, Loss,
and Letting Go*

HENDRICKSON PUBLISHERS

Caring for Our Aging Parents:
Lessons in Love, Loss, and Letting Go

© 2016 Hendrickson Publishers Marketing, LLC
P. O. Box 3473
Peabody, Massachusetts 01961-3473
www.hendrickson.com

ISBN 978-1-61970-835-8

Scripture quotations contained herein are taken from the Holy Bible, New International Version®, NIV®. Copyright © 1973, 1978, 1984, 2011 by Biblica, Inc.™ Used by permission of Zondervan. All rights reserved worldwide. www.zondervan.com The "NIV" and "New International Version" are trademarks registered in the United States Patent and Trademark Office by Biblica, Inc.™

Printed in the United States of America

First Printing—October 2016

Library of Congress Cataloging-in-Publication Data

Names: Howe, Michele, author.
Title: Caring for our aging parents : lessons in love, loss, and
   letting go / Michele Howe.
Description: Peabody, MA : Hendrickson Publishers, 2016.
Identifiers: LCCN 2016033379 | ISBN 9781619708358
   (alk. paper)
Subjects: LCSH: Adult children of aging parents--Religious life. |
   Aging parents--Care--Religious aspects--Christianity. |
   Caregivers--Religious life.
Classification: LCC BV4910.9 .H69 2016 | DDC 248.8/4--dc23
   LC record available at https://lccn.loc.gov/2016033379

To my father-in-law,
James Leland Howe, Sr.,
who taught me the meaning of a "good death."

Contents

Acknowledgements

Like every other author I know, I recognize (with gratitude) that it takes a skill set far beyond my own ability to fashion my words into a book that invites savvy consumers to first pick up (or click on) and read. Every single time someone takes the time to read my work, I feel deeply humbled because as an author and a book reviewer, I know how many excellent resources there are to choose from these days.

But right now, I want to give my thanks to my agent, Les Stobbe, who never wavers in supporting me both personally and professionally. Les, you always have my back, and I'm honored to be part of Mr. Stobbe's Neighborhood. May it increase in strength and number every year.

Receiving a new book contract never loses its thrill. Never. Ever. So my sincerest thanks go to editorial director Patricia Anders for giving my proposal a read and then giving me the good news that I can once again count myself among the fine authors at Hendrickson Publishers. Again, the English language falls far short as I'm wondering how many ways I can say thank you!

To marketing coordinator Meghan Rusick, I love all your fabulous ideas (so keep them coming!). Whenever I see your name in my e-mail inbox, I perk up anticipating the good things that await me. Thank you for lending your expertise to my project.

Finally, I want to say thank you to the entire Hendrickson editorial, design, and production team for making me one happy, happy, happy author. What else can I say but thank you, thank you, thank you!

 *Introduction*

The birth of any book comes when real-life experiences meet a real-life opportunity to communicate lessons learned. *Caring for Our Aging Parents* is no exception to this rule. In all honesty, the first time our family was suddenly made responsible for caring for someone we loved, we didn't do a very good job. We did, however, learn a lot. Some years later, we had another chance to serve an elderly family member we loved dearly, and we put to use the lessons we had learned to do a better job—and what a world of difference that made (to us and to our loved one) the second time around.

The irony in caregiving is that to do it well, we need practice. Lots and lots of practice. Though it sounds rather callous, the hard truth is that unless we do something time and time again, we can't master the skills required to do it effectively. This theory applies to serving those we love no matter what the individual circumstance looks like. It really didn't matter how much passion we put into serving when we first attempted to take care of our elderly relative—and in all honesty, we did our heartfelt best. We stumbled, we fell, and we routinely came up short in the process. Looking back, it was disheartening.

Some books are years in the making. This is one of those books. The backstory behind this text, *Caring for Our*

Aging Parents, began about ten years ago when we were suddenly (and quite unpreparedly) thrust into caring for our elderly neighbor/relative. At that time, my husband and I were still parenting our four teenagers and life was hectic (spell "Hectic" with a capital "H"). Between running around to our children's never-ending events and caring for their ongoing needs in the home, I felt I couldn't have taken on any other responsibility large or small and done justice to it. But the Lord had other plans (doesn't he always?).

We had spent the last twenty-seven years of our married lives settled here in the country (in my husband's grandparents' home) and we loved it. The surrounding fields of seasonal crops, the Lake Erie shoreline right down the street, and the boat marinas on three sides of us made our home heavenly to us. As folks who value the wide-open spaces, we also treasured the fact that we had only one neighbor and he was a gem. Bill, my husband's elderly second cousin, was an only child, as well as a lifelong bachelor with no children of his own. He was also our neighbor and had pretty much adopted our four kids as his own grandchildren from early on. He was an honest-to-goodness genuine farmer, game hunter/fisherman, live-off-the-land type of guy. Bill was independent, self-sufficient, and had loads of friends. We loved him. Our kids loved him. Bill was always there if we needed anything and vice versa. It was a very companionable relationship that we shared.

Bill's health remained robust until he turned seventy. Then during the next five years, he was in and out of the hospital more times than I care to remember. This once healthy outdoorsman contracted seemingly every major illness under the sun. It all started with colon cancer, then diabetes, then Parkinson's, then open heart surgery, and then another cancer. Add to these the personal (and lingering) indignities of almost constant urinary issues that required catheters, and you can imagine how difficult it became for this once proudly independent man to handle his health problems and continue to live in his home alone.

In the aftermath of each of Bill's health crises, we took on different roles in caregiving for him. At first, Bill's primary recovery from his first cancer surgery was spent in a rehab facility. We were close enough that we visited him almost daily. Between my husband and me, we took care of his home, his dog, his bills, his medicines, his groceries, and so on. After each recovery, Bill repeatedly returned to live in his own home, even though at times this wasn't the safest of environments for him. Back and forth, between the hospital and a rehab/nursing home, Bill rallied from one illness to another for five painful years. Then, during a relatively minor medical procedure, Bill passed away quite unexpectedly in the hospital. After he died, we did a lot of reflecting about what we did right and what we did wrong. In truth, there were more "wrongs" than "rights."

When I say "wrong," I mean that some of the caregiving choices we made out of inexperience and naivete caused much upset in our marriage and in our immediate family. In our desire to help Bill, we neglected to think through other possible options that would have prevented burnout on our part and still met his needs. We did "right" in wanting to help Bill the best way we knew how, but we did "wrong" in some of our methodology.

The Lord, however, sometimes gives us second chances for do-overs. Several years after Bill passed away, we found out that my father-in-law, James, was ill. I still recall sitting at the after-funeral dinner for my husband's grandfather when my husband's father announced that he had been given the dire news of esophageal cancer. Too quickly, James was in daily radiation treatments, and attending a myriad of doctor appointments, all while his pain level escalated rapidly. As we grieved what we knew was coming because he had been given only a few months to live, my husband and I took stock of the all the mistakes we had made with Bill and tried to choose more wisely this time around. Born of our prior exhausting experience, we now had knowledge and information to better prepare a smoother caregiving plan for my dying father-in-law.

Thankfully, as soon as the family heard the news of his illness, everyone offered to help divide up the caregiving responsibilities. Nobody had to take on the solo role of "hero caregiver" and manage his care 24/7. Rather, we all did our part, and I truly believe James rejoiced in the amount of attention and love he received during those last precious months of his life. He passed away a brief five months after being diagnosed, but during those final weeks, I saw a formerly fearful man transformed from the inside out. As I was able to spend a good deal of time in waiting rooms with him, I even now consider those last conversations we shared as some of the most precious in our over thirty-year relationship. God was able to pack much love, goodness, and healing into those months. Maybe one of the most lasting treasures is that we all recall those moments with him without any of the regret that had tainted our last memories of Cousin Bill.

As I contemplate the difference between our first caregiving experiences with Bill with that of my father-in-law, I am still amazed how polar opposite they were in every conceivable way. They were similar in that we lost two men we loved, but different in how smoothly the second caregiving season was in comparison to the first. From these two experiences, I realized how ill prepared I had been to take good care of these fine men. Thus all these residual thoughts and emotions have provided yet another excellent motive for developing this book that brings together a variety of experiences lived out by men and women in diverse situations and scenarios.

Each story found within these pages will offer readers practical wisdom gleaned from serving an elderly loved one up close and personal. Looking around, I recognize that loving others through to the end of their lives is frequently smattered with real regrets. My own motivation in telling my story (and others' stories) is to learn from my mistakes (as well as others') and approach the whole caregiving role smarter, wiser, and more effectively the next time around. I cannot allow myself the selfish luxury of future (or present) inaction simply because I made mistakes in the past. And neither can you.

Are you ready to journey along with those who experienced some ups and downs in their caregiving history? I sure am. Let's get ready—and then get busy giving care in a way that brings honor to the Lord and to our loved ones.

Chapter 1

Change Is Inevitable

Praise be to the God and Father of our Lord Jesus
Christ, the Father of compassion and the God of
all comfort, who comforts us in all our troubles,
so that we can comfort those in any trouble with
the comfort we ourselves receive from God.

2 Corinthians 1:3–4

*If God has made your cup sweet, drink it with grace;
or even if He has made it bitter, drink
it in communion with Him.*

Oswald Chambers

When Melissa sat herself down on the long flight eastward from California, she wondered if she would fall apart when she got to the hospital. Her mother had just endured a massive heart attack and combined with all of her other medical conditions, the doctors didn't hold much hope. Melissa closed her eyes and considered everything her folks had been through in the past five years. They had buried one child, Melissa's older brother, after his long battle with cancer. They had moved from their bustling home in the suburbs to an assisted-living condo that was part of a larger retirement community. Their beloved dog was hit by a car and died at the scene. Then Mom's health really took a turn for the worse.

Melissa thought about each of these events and how any one of them could trigger mild depression. She felt down-and-out, imagining how her folks must be feeling. Hoping to keep her emotions to a minimum when she finally got to see her mother, Melissa prayed she would have the right words of comfort to encourage her parents. Looking at the landscape below, Melissa began recalling her parents' wonderful legacy of faith and service to each other and to their community.

Growing up, Melissa was never taken by surprise when a guest (or two) showed up with Dad for dinner. Mom, for her part, never seemed to mind. They were both terrific examples of showing hospitality—although Melissa remembered feeling jealous of the time they spent helping other people out. She knew it was childish to feel this way. But there it was: a younger Melissa hungered for her parents' love and attention more than she wanted them spreading their goodwill around town. Today, as an adult, Melissa was grateful for her parents in every way possible.

A few hours later, Melissa entered the hospital and went directly to the ICU. What she saw shocked her in the best way possible. There sat her father holding her mother's hand while he read from the Bible. He placed a small wafer in her mouth before popping another into his own. Finally, he tenderly held her mother's head so she could swallow a sip of the grape juice. Then they both closed their eyes while Melissa's father prayed a prayer of thanksgiving to God. Melissa held back because she didn't want to interrupt this holy moment. As she stood there in the shadows, Melissa realized something. Her parents had founded their entire life on making Jesus first. And now, in her mother's final days, why did she think they would do anything different?

Sometimes when we watch people we love suffer, we wrongly assume they are experiencing the same feelings of sorrow and regret and pain that we are as we observe them. But we forget that God promises his grace and strength to the one who is suffering—not to those who are merely watching. Yes, he gives us all grace to play our parts in this life. However, his word says that he gives his grace as needed. There is something to this "dying grace."

Let's not short-circuit what God plans to do in the lives of our loved ones even in their final days and hours. Before he calls them home, he may teach them some of their most important life lessons. As bystanders to suffering, we're called to support, pray, and simply be there. As Melissa happily discovered, God was doing something beautiful in her folks as they shared communion together in the ICU. It didn't matter that her mother couldn't speak or pray aloud; her father did it for both of them. That poignant moment stuck with Melissa and it changed her. Today, she isn't nearly so surprised when God shows up in his glory and goodness in even the most unexpected places. Amen and amen.

Take-away Action Thought

I want to stop assuming that I know how
life's difficult moments are going to unfold.
Instead, I need to be on the watch for
God's mercy and grace everywhere I go.

My Heart's Cry to You, O Lord

Father, I am in awe of how you totally transformed a meeting I was dreading into a moment that was beyond beautiful. I believe I was part of a holy happening as I watched something akin to the divine transpire in front of me. I was so stunned by this turn of events. Help me to stop being surprised when you show up in unexpected ways and unexpected places. You continue to demonstrate your supernatural comfort and care for my family through all of life and on to death. Let me never forget what I've witnessed as two suffering Christians worshipped you with all their hearts. Amen.

Chapter 2

Role Reversal

I was young and now I am old,
    yet I have never seen the righteous forsaken
    or their children begging bread.
They are always generous and lend freely;
    their children will be a blessing.

Psalm 37:25–26

If you and I are going to meet the needs of others, we must not view people as interruptions. We must be willing to see them from God's perspective, and we must be willing to give up some of our own time to help meet their needs.

Anne Graham Lotz

Nannette is a young widow who lives in the same town as her elderly parents. She sees to it that her mother and father can live safely in their own home for as long as possible. Nannette makes sure they take regular baths, brush their teeth twice a day, and get their medicines on time. She also oversees their eating habits and lately she has paid for Meals on Wheels to come every day to provide them with dinner.

Nannette is still working full time at a local hospital as a nurse, and her own four children and grandchildren often beg for more time with her. Nannette sometimes has to expertly juggle her schedule to fit in the caregiving responsibilities she has taken on and still have time for her beloved kids and grandchildren. And her folks don't make it easy for Nannette. They complain she isn't around enough to take them to the movies, to the mall, to the theater. In short, they truly want Nannette to be their social network on top of being their caregiver.

In the real world, we know that Nannette cannot fulfill everyone's expectations and still maintain her own health and sanity. Eventually, Nannette's resolve to be everything to everyone would dissolve into a heap—as would she. Because Nannette is a professional health-care provider, she knows better than to make even the attempt at sacrificing more time each week to become her parents' sole social outlet. And she has told them so.

Nannette wisely put things in the right order. She assessed her parents' needs from a professional standpoint and made changes and adjustments as necessary. Then she contacted organizations that specialize in serving the elderly. Nannette keeps a close eye on her parents' ever-changing health, but she also encourages them to seek out meaningful activities and outlets at the local senior center and through the YMCA, which offers numerous exercise classes and activities for older members. Rather than burn herself out, Nannette views handling her parents' care as a long-term marathon proposition. It's not a sprint. Nannette has erected healthy boundaries for herself and her parents—so that even though their relationship is now re-versed in many ways, it can remain a cordial one.

❧

It is so refreshing to hear about the way in which Nan-nette chose to handle her parents' needs. She wisely began to look at their lives from a big picture perspective. Then she jotted down their most necessary and primary needs: food, shelter, safety, cleanliness, medicines, and doctor's care. Next, she made a list of what she knew they wanted from her that she didn't have time or the energy to give: social outlet, running them all over town, taking them to movies/theater, and so on. Once Nannette separated needs from secondary wants, it made her task much simpler.

Nannette decided what she could reasonably do over a long stretch of time and then organized her calendar to include these tasks. Then she started making phone calls to set up other agencies to fill in the gaps. While Nan-nette understands that her parents would prefer to have her doing everything for them, she has kindly made clear what she can and cannot commit to doing. On days when Nannette begins to feel guilty for not having the time or energy for everyone, she steps back and reminds herself that it does indeed take a village to raise a child (or care for one's parents).

Take-away Action Thought

When I'm tempted to take full and overwhelming responsibility for my parents' care, I will stop and remind myself that overdoing anything is the fastest way to burnout. I will also discipline myself to separate real needs from wants and communicate those differences to my parents.

My Heart's Cry to You, O Lord

Help me to use common sense as well as divine wisdom as I approach my caregiving role with my parents, especially as I know they would love to have me all to themselves. Please remind them that I have a family of my own, a job, and many other pressing tasks on my plate. I don't want to grow resentful toward them when they take for granted all that I already do. Help me to remember that my parents are viewing life from a different perspective from my own. Give me the compassion I need to give loving care on a consistent basis, no matter what their response is to me. Amen.

Chapter 3

They're My Parents Too

Refrain from anger and turn from wrath;
do not fret—it leads only to evil.

Psalm 37:8

*What is a relationship? The intersection of the
stories of two people. The problem is that an awful
lot of carnage takes place at this intersection.*

Tim Lane and Paul David Tripp

When I noticed my good friend Annie breathing in and
out with deliberate breaths, I knew trouble was brewing.
Annie, my almost always entirely unflappable friend, took
a lot grief from her sisters. None of whom, let the record
stand, took even thirty minutes a month to check up on
their aging parents who had moved to an assisted-living
condo. Annie, the middle sister of three, did everything for
her folks. Most of the time Annie focused on caring for her
parents in spite of the fact that she knew full well her two
sisters could be (should be) helping out. What galled Annie
the most wasn't the work itself—it was how her sisters' lack
of caring hurt their parents.

Annie could almost predict when her mother or father might bring up the touchy topic of her sisters. Most generally, it was right before a family birthday, an anniversary, or a holiday. They tried so hard not to let it show how much they missed Annie's sisters' participation (or lack thereof . . .). For her part, Annie struggled with intermittent anger. There were many long nights preceding any type of family gathering when Annie spent rehearsing how and what she might say that just possibly could convince her sisters to join them in the festivities. It was shameful. That's what Annie thought about the entire pitiful situation.

Sometimes, before she could stop herself, Annie would start reliving the emotional weeks prior to her parents' move to the assisted-living facility. Annie never would have believed it of her sisters before she had witnessed that fiasco of trying to divvy up all the odds and ends their folks didn't want to take with them. Annie still gets the shudders as she replays those heated, adversarial conversations she watched unfold between her two sisters when both wanted the same particular item. It was scary.

Still, Annie realizes she cannot get caught up in her sisters' pettiness—not when there are a million things to do, and each task has her name written on it. Instead, Annie frequently reminds herself (or calls a friend like me who gently reminds her) that she is only responsible for her part before the Lord. And from my point of view, Annie is doing just fine. In fact, there are few people I'd rather have in my corner than this wonderful servant-hearted soul.

16

If the phrase "They're my parents too!" makes you cringe when you hear it, you're absolutely right on. That particular sentiment isn't too far afield from little children squabbling over their newest toy, favorite snack, or the television remote. It remains a cringe-worthy sentiment no matter who does the speaking. Unfortunately, the unsavory situation of fighting over aging parents' material goods, their money, or even their good favor happens more often than most folks realize.

I've always maintained that the real you comes out at weddings and funerals, and the days prior to both. People truly do reveal what they treasure through a display of their words, their actions, and what they are willing to fight to possess. As Annie experienced with her sisters, many families contain a smattering of faithful sons and daughters who are willing to step up and get busy caring for their aged parents. And then, there are the other family members who do nothing and whom no one sees until the house is sold and the will is read. It's despicable from any perspective.

Like Annie, many responsible and loving adult children have to come to terms with whom they are dealing—not just their younger sister or older brother. They need to candidly recognize the character (and flaws) of their siblings. It's not easy. It's not comfortable. It's not a stress-free scenario. Many families are torn apart by the obvious greedy gusto demonstrated by a few.

Wisely, Annie recognized early on that she wouldn't be able to count on her sisters for either assistance or support. So a wise woman in that situation does what she needs to: she gathers her troops in other ways. Annie didn't try to handle every responsibility for her folks. She did, however, make a list of reliable people and organizations to call on for tasks she wasn't able to take on. By doing so, Annie had more energy and far more emotional reserves to love her parents.

She also worked daily to keep the slate as clean as possible between herself, her expectations, and her sisters. No doubt, there were still difficult moments, sometimes difficult days. But overall, Annie was at peace with God, with herself—and even with her irresponsible siblings. Unlike her sisters, Annie cultivated a longer view of life. She knew her folks wouldn't be around forever, and she wanted to have no regrets after they passed on. As I said earlier, there are few people I'd rather have in my corner than this wonderful servant-hearted soul.

Take-away Action Thought

When I am tempted to nurse anger and bitterness over the lack of caring by my siblings, I will get down on my knees and stay there until I've thoroughly handed the situation back to the Lord. I realize I am thoroughly unable to make my siblings care about our parents, so I need God to help me let go of any anger festering inside.

My Heart's Cry to You, O Lord

You alone know how angry I feel when my family fails to step up and take care of our folks. Lord, help me to let go of every expectation I have and help me focus on doing what I can do to serve. Show me practical ways to ease the discomfort of aging in my parents. Provide me with ideas that will bring blessing to their lives as they get feebler. I know that some days are more difficult than others (for them and for me). Protect my heart and guide my mind to think on only what is true, noble, right, pure, lovely, admirable, excellent, or praiseworthy. Amen.

Chapter 4

Tough Love

"I will never leave you nor forsake you."
Joshua 1:5

Worry and fear say that the world is threatening and you are alone. But when the kingdom of heaven pierces the earth, God is establishing his control in a new way. Now that the King has come, you will never be alone.
Edward Welch

There are moments you never forget, and there are moments you wish you could wipe from your mind forever. This was one of those times. I was sitting in a conference room, waiting for our neighbor Bill to be brought in for evaluation. He was recovering from major surgery (a cancerous tumor had been removed from the outer lining of his colon) and a few weeks' stint in rehab. The discussion for the day was whether or not Bill was strong enough to move back home. There were social workers, medical personnel, and various other rehab staff members sitting around that table with me.

When they wheeled Bill into the room, he was all smiles. Of course, Bill assumed this was his release day from the rehabilitation center. In fact, from the way Bill looked and how merrily he was conversing with the folks around him, it suddenly occurred to me that Bill wasn't in any way aware that this wasn't a release meeting. Rather, it was a conversation between a group of professionals who had yet to decide if he was able to live at home again now—or ever.

My heart sank as this realization hit home. Before I could even try to prepare Bill for what might happen, the meeting had started. Around the room, each person responsible for Bill's care referred to their written notes while the others listened attentively. For my part, I was so mindful of the fact that Bill honestly believed he was getting released that very afternoon, I had a hard time concentrating. Finally, they looked at me and asked about the living arrangements:

"Does Bill live with you?"

Their question caught me off guard. "Excuse me?"

"Does Bill reside in your home?"

"No, he is our neighbor. Bill lives alone in his house."

Stunned silence.

Each person looked around at the others until finally someone voiced what everyone what thinking: "We were under the impression that Bill lived in your home."

Sadly, I shook my head because I knew where this was heading. The fact that Bill lived alone meant he would not be released that day—or any day soon. Even with our help, even with nurses coming in daily, even with meals and a cleaning service, Bill simply wasn't strong enough to be alone in his own home.

For some minutes it was deathly quiet before the social worker broke the silence and looked at Bill and said, "We really believe it's in your best interest to stay here until you're stronger and more mobile."

When I mustered up the courage to look at Bill, he was crying. Big, rolling tears were sliding down his cheeks. I gulped back my own. I still remember feeling a huge lump in my throat as he looked at me to as if to say, "Tell them something . . . anything . . . so they will let me come home." I couldn't. It wasn't safe for Bill to be alone yet.

I felt like a betrayer who was leaving a loved one behind on the battlefield. I sat there thinking fast and furiously. Was there some way we could work it out so that Bill could safely come home? There wasn't. Not yet. Certainly not today. To be honest, I kept wishing my husband had been available to take that meeting in my stead. I felt all my emotions bubbling over, and the motherly part of me wanted to "fix" the situation in favor of getting Bill home no matter what the risks. The other part of me, the rational side, knew better. Getting Bill home was one thing—keeping him there safely was another.

So on that day, I couldn't give Bill what he wanted more than anything else in the world—a ride home. Instead, I sat with him for a while after the meeting ended and tried to encourage him to keep working hard in physical therapy, to keep walking the halls with his walker, and to listen to whatever instructions his physician gave him. Was it enough? Not nearly. But on that dismal afternoon, it was the best I had to offer.

❦

As parents, we realize the value of tough love and that if we really love our children, we don't always give them what they want. What feels especially unnatural, though, is applying tough love to an aging relative. Everything about that afternoon felt wrong. I asked myself a myriad of questions as I sat at that table where Bill's current fate was literally being decided. I didn't like it one bit. Over and over, I questioned whether or not I was acting for Bill's benefit or my own. Because the truth was, it was easier for us to have Bill cared for in rehab. Once I thought through the daily implications of Bill returning home alone, I knew without a doubt that he wasn't strong enough yet.

Still, as difficult as it is to tell a toddler no when they ask for something that will hurt them, it was a hundred times harder to say no to Bill that day. And yet, it was the most loving decision I could make, knowing he wasn't able to navigate being home alone, night and day, anytime soon. Eventually, Bill did come back home. If memory serves, it was a few weeks after that initial roundtable meeting. And when Bill did arrive at his doorstep, he was able to walk through on his own two feet. Oh, glorious, happy day!

That day of decision-making, however, forever altered how I viewed caregiving. It made me keenly sensitive to how seriously I needed to take the whole concept of "giving care" to another person. Watching how Bill's face fell (as well as his tears) made me conscious of the weight of trust Bill had placed upon our shoulders, and the trust between us. It was heart-wrenching to see the disappointment in his eyes and know I was partly responsible for it. And yet, I couldn't have made any other choice. Like so many times in life when a crucial decision is being made, we have to set aside our emotions and reason through to the best and most loving choice available. And it's never a pain-free scenario for anyone involved.

Take-away Action Thought

When I need to make a decision that tears at
my heart and emotions, I will purposefully step
back, be quiet, pray, and then decide what is
best in the long run. I need to think through
the possible risks of these difficult decisions
and not give in to my ever-changing emotions.

My Heart's Cry to You, O Lord

Today I had to step up in a new capacity and make a
decision to protect my loved one. It was one of the most
difficult moments in my life. As I was asked to choose, I
was aware that I was hurting my loved one by my decision.
Even though I know it was done in love, I feel the weight
of their pain on me. In truth, I feel like it's my fault they
are hurting now. Help me to bear this burden of caregiving,
even when it gets rough and I'd rather pass the decision-
making on to someone else. I know you have called me to
serve my loved one in this capacity, and I surely need your
wisdom, grace, and love to do it well. Amen.

Chapter 5

Love and Respect Defined

"Love your neighbor as yourself."
Matthew 19:19

*The great women theologians I have come across
cultivated the habit of using their theology in the
here and now. What set these women apart—kept
them from sinking when everything else was going
down and strengthened them to lend a hand to
others—was their unblinking focus on God.*
Carolyn Custis James

I still remember how my neck and shoulders ached
after yet another tense discussion about how to best care
for Bill. My husband had his firm convictions. I had mine.
Sometimes (a lot of times) these two perspectives never
met. Truth be told, there were countless occasions when we
were divided about what our roles should look like as Bill's
neighbor and relative. While we both wanted to do what was
best for Bill and tried to give him all the help he needed
through those five years when his health was declining, day
to day our individual plans played out differently.

My husband, who had spent hours alone with Bill over the years as our children were growing up, felt that Bill had invested so much in him personally. Bill was a man who never missed a visitation, a funeral, or making daily trips to see a friend in the hospital. He was brought up to honor his friends and family and to "be there" for them in sickness and in health. My husband watched Bill put himself out there time and again. Then when folks we knew were sick, dying, or had passed away, my husband took up the same mantle of care and concern as Bill had done. In that way, my husband observed Bill's care for others and then modeled it himself.

When Bill could no longer actively go visit others, my husband sometimes went in his stead; at other times, he took our kids along with him. My husband became passionate about setting the same giving example to our children that Bill had shown by demonstrating care for others in need. He felt it was our responsibility to pass on this heritage of being there for people who were hurting, sick, and grieving. I agreed with him. Until I didn't.

At times, I had the same desire to go and be present for others, but was neck deep handling my responsibilities with our children. It was during those exhausting moments when I felt totally depleted that we argued about how much involvement I could reasonably expect to take on caregiving for Bill. It wasn't that my husband was unaware of how torn I was between my current job of raising four kids (and everything associated with that ongoing role) and serving Bill. My husband's heart cried out to demonstrate love and respect for Bill, but he had a wife (me) who was consumed by the caregiving of her children. We agreed we wanted to take care of Bill but that we just didn't have the experience or the resources to do it well. Thus tension erupted frequently between us.

Whenever anyone says that caregiving is a joy and a privilege, believe them. But also realize that in the real world caregivers get sick, burned out, overwhelmed, and depressed because the to-do list never ends. I would love to say that over time my husband and I completely worked through our differences of how to adequately care for Bill, but we didn't—as least not until well after he had passed away. It took us time and some distance (from the caregiving task) to honestly look back and learn from our mistakes.

Today, we have a much healthier and more balanced perspective on caregiving. It involves respecting each other's decisions, choices, perspectives, and limitations— and doing so in a loving manner. I know when I've reached my end-capacity for giving and serving. I also recognize the telltale signs when I'm getting burned out: my patience drops to zero; I am easily upset and irritated; I cry; I withdraw. These are my "tells" that I need to step back, re-evaluate, and take some rest. My husband's "tells" are different from mine, but I've learned to cue into them and suggest he take a break as well. I jokingly remind my husband that even Bill used to take a nap every afternoon in between his social visits.

❧

Looking back from a distance that has erased much of the emotional intensity from caregiving, I can see that although my husband and I didn't realize it at the time, our then differing perspectives were helpful in balancing out each other. My husband was so focused on being present for Bill that he didn't look for others who could have stepped in to assist us during those five years. I was so focused on raising my kids that I felt resentful when Bill needed more of "me" than I could give.

Hindsight is twenty-twenty. We cannot alter the past, but we can learn from the mistakes we made in it. Today, when a new request for caregiving arises, an almost automatic list of creative ways to meet that need runs right through my brain. Interestingly, it doesn't always include me getting involved firsthand. Sometimes, I locate a professional organization that specializes in meeting a specific need. Other times, I connect the needy with just the right need-meeter. In every case, I try to stop, think, and pray before saying yes.

Over the years, I've discovered that while some needs might be brought to me, God may be using me as the connector, not the one to give the actual care. I've learned that when I take on too much—because I do care—nothing (not even well-intentioned caregiving) gets done well. I've also learned that when God calls me to a task, he always, always enables me to complete it as I depend upon him and his ongoing strength and grace. We serve one another in love. We treat one another with respect. We rely on God for the strength to do both.

Take-away Action Thought

During those moments when exhaustion overwhelms me, I will retreat to a quiet place and listen to God's voice. I also need to listen well to my family members as we seek to take care of our extended family and not become frustrated if we choose to demonstrate our care in different ways.

My Heart's Cry to You, O Lord

You know how I long to fulfill your charge to love our neighbors as ourselves. In my heart of hearts, I truly want to live that principle out day by day. But you also know how overwhelmed I feel most of the time. I am tired, Lord. Tired, weary, and worn down by the nonstop demands on me and my time. Help me to step back and prayerfully consider what I know you've called me to do today. Give me the wisdom to let go of the nonessential responsibilities that eat up my time and energy. I need to draw closer still to you when you place a burden of service before me. Give me everything I need to lovingly take care of those you've placed around me and to do it with your good grace. Amen.

Chapter 6

When Finances Become Deal Breakers

"Do not worry about tomorrow, for tomorrow will worry
about itself. Each day has enough trouble of its own."
Matthew 6:34

*God does not give twenty years of grace
today. Rather, He gives it day by day.*
Jerry Bridges

When Sandy filled up her gas tank for the third time
in five days, she started to panic. Sure, she could charge
it. But the bill still came due at the end of every month.
As a longtime single mother, Sandy used to charge everything and anything to put off the inevitable. After about ten
years of barely making it and feeling sick about how much
interest she was paying by submitting only the minimum
amount on each bill, she met with a financial advisor who
put her on a budget. Some fifteen years later, Sandy is still
either paying with cash or paying her credit card in full
every month. Freedom!

Sandy learned her lesson the hard way in a lot of ways
over the years. She didn't want to go back to those early
days when her stomach tied up in knots every time a bill

arrived in the mail. But with her recently added responsibility of running to her folks' house some fifty miles away several times a week, she knew she didn't have enough in her gas budget to cover this additional cost indefinitely. Not to mention the fact that her parents saved up all their errands for the days when Sandy could drive them around town.

Money had always been a sore subject in Sandy's home growing up. Though her father worked long hours at a factory, it barely met their basic needs, and each of Sandy's siblings got part-time jobs after school as soon as they were of age. Sandy knew better than to ask her folks to help chip in for her gas money. Recoiling at the memory of one conversation she had witnessed with her brother years ago made her vow to never, ever ask her folks for any kind of monetary help. Even though it made sense for Sandy's folks to offer to pay for her gas to come to help them, Sandy refused to get her hopes up. Instead, she opted for trying to cut back in other areas, which she knew full well would eventually cause her to feel resentment toward her parents when she sat down to pay her bills.

A good friend challenged her on this decision after Sandy explained her dilemma. Her friend wisely said, "You have a choice here: either you summon up the courage to ask for gas money, or you'll find yourself becoming resentful every time you struggle to come up with extra money on your own. Remember, you're doing your folks a big service driving that far three times a week and sacrificing your time, energy, and your wallet to do so. God values service, but not at the expense of the relationship." Wise words that I'm happy to report Sandy heeded as she sat in her car and prayed for the strength to ask for financial help to continue making those long drives three times a week. Happily, her parents completely understood Sandy's dilemma and started writing her a check for gas money every week.

Money. Money. Money. It seems the entire world revolves around cold hard cash or its equivalent. As Sandy discovered, it was fine and dandy to want to help out her elderly parents by driving that fifty miles three times a week, but it took a financial toll on her pocketbook almost immediately. In a perfect world, Sandy would not have had to ask her folks to pitch in the difference for gas money. In the real world, Sandy had a difficult decision to make, and one she dreaded. With her parents' attitude toward money (because there never seemed to be enough), they tended to be tightfisted—even when acts of generosity were warranted. Recalling the rebuff her brother received at an earlier date caused her even more anxiety. If she had been able to afford it, Sandy would have gladly paid the extra amount every week. But perhaps God had orchestrated something better—something with a longer lasting lesson in mind for both Sandy and her parents.

A healthy relationship consists of two parties who give and take with loads of grace and large doses of generosity. It's all about putting someone's needs above our own. Sandy was all about giving without any strings attached, but God allowed her monetary limitations to force her into having a conversation that may have been more about Sandy's parents than her. Maybe, maybe not. What Sandy learned was this: God doesn't want her fretting about tomorrow's needs. He promises to care for her as she cares for her folks. What exactly that may look like in real-life terms is anyone's guess. But most important, Sandy knows from experience that God is always faithful.

Take-away Action Thought

When faced with having a conversation
I'd rather not take part in, I will place my
hope, trust, and outcome into God's faithful
hands before I begin to speak. I need
to view my difficulties from a long-term
perspective and handle each small conflict
as it happens so I do not become resentful.

My Heart's Cry to You, O Lord

Father, you know that in my heart of hearts I would gladly give to my parents. But I'm not in the financial position to do so. I realize I can help them, but I cannot afford to put out cash week after week. Help me to be humble enough to admit this to them and ask for their help. I hate asking for help. Maybe this is part of my problem—my independence is not healthy. You created us as interdependent on each other and wholly dependent upon you. Help me to swallow my pride, ask for help, and then leave the outcome in your hands. You know my motive is pure and I'm not doing this for any personal gain. Amen.

Chapter 7

Finding Common Ground

Make every effort to keep the unity of the
Spirit through the bond of peace.

Ephesians 4:3

*People imagine that dying to self makes one
miserable. But it is just the opposite. It is the
refusal to die to self that makes one miserable.*

Roy Hession

You'd never guess that Grace and her mother were related. No one who knew these two oh-so-different women
would ever think they came from the same family. Grace,
my friend, is a generous, kindhearted, servant-minded
mother of five whose budgeting skills put mine to shame.
Grace's mother is a wealthy, social-climber widow whose
main concern in life is being regularly named on the society page of her city's newspaper. These two women are so
opposite in their lifestyle and life aims that they've never
enjoyed a close mother-daughter relationship.

That is, until Grace's mother broke her hip last fall and
needed hip replacement surgery. Grace quickly realized
that the years were over of trying to tolerate each other's

differences. Both women were going to be seeing lots of each other, at least until Grace's mother got the go-ahead to drive again. So, being the faithful daughter that she is, Grace now squeezes three afternoons into her already packed to overflowing schedule for caregiving duties to her mother. On Mondays, Grace stops by her mother's palatial home and picks up her mother's list for groceries and other supplies. On Wednesdays, Grace cleans and does her mother's laundry. On Fridays, Grace takes her mother to any doctor's appointments she has scheduled and then out for dinner.

Grace realizes this extra commitment won't last forever—and for that she is grateful. But during her triweekly visits, Grace has also come to realize something else: Her mother is aging quickly and won't be around forever. This revelation has caused Grace to begin asking some hard questions about their relationship. She's wondering if after all these years there isn't some way to bridge the deep gap between them before it's too late.

When we talked about her dilemma, it was clear that Grace and her mother had nothing in common. They even approached their faith differently. So we prayed that God would somehow show Grace even a small area of common interest upon which to build a closer relationship. After a few weeks of fervent prayer, Grace called me to say she finally realized something they both enjoyed: black and white movies from the forties and fifties. Who knew?

Apparently even Grace had forgotten that her mother was an old movie buff until she stopped by one afternoon and her mother was watching one on her big-screen TV. Revelation! Immediately, Grace realized this was something they both could appreciate together—just like real friends; just like a real mother and daughter.

✼

Growing up in the same family home doesn't necessarily mean having much in common. As Grace and her mother realized early on in life, they simply had different tastes, different priorities, and even a different faith. Over the years, Grace continued to reach out to her mother by inviting her over for dinner, asking her to join them for special events with their children, most especially on holidays. Sadly, more often than not, Grace's mother had made other plans. Of course, this lack of closeness took its toll over time, and Grace often felt sad she didn't have a mother who wanted to be an intimate part of her family.

Grace's children, too, felt the brunt of this distance. As an adult, Grace and her husband frequently discussed the ever-broadening divide between Grace and her mother. But what to do? They'd tried everything they could think of to draw her mother in, but to no avail. Interestingly, Grace now believes it took that serious fall and subsequent surgery to immobilize her mother to get her mother's attention. As Grace continued to show up and serve her mother over those many weeks and months, something in her mother began to soften. At first, it was a little comment here or there. Then a rare smile shone on her face. Finally, when Grace issued another invitation for the upcoming holiday dinner at their home, her mother accepted and even thanked Grace. Will wonders never cease? Never let it be said that the power of small persistent kindnesses don't leave their mark—and sometimes these same small kindnesses completely tumble formerly impenetrable walls between people.

Take-away Action Thought

When I become discouraged and am tempted to give up on a relationship that has been always difficult, I will call to mind the Scripture that says, "With God anything is possible!"

My Heart's Cry to You, O Lord

I sorely need you to give me your divine wisdom when dealing with my difficult relative. Lord, you know we have nothing in common. Never have we enjoyed the same things in life, and it feels as though we are always at odds with one another. This has to change. The older my parent grows, the more I feel a sense of urgency to make things right between us. Help me, give me just the right words to bridge the gap. Show me how to love her in a way so that she feels loved. Clothe me with a gentle and humble spirit always. And in all ways, empower me to set aside my rights and find a way to love. Amen.

Chapter 8

Adjusting Expectations

Each of you should look not only to your own
interests, but also to the interests of others.

Philippians 2:4

*Needing God but not always wanting God, we
expect others to take the place of God in our lives,
depending on them to guide our decisions, to love
us continuously and unconditionally, to provide
for us emotionally, physically, socially, totally.*

Nancy Leigh DeMoss

Joe had been on the receiving end of good things from
his elderly neighbor Frank for as long as he had lived in
his home. Over twenty-five years had passed since Joe
and his family moved out to the country and next door to
Frank. Joe often remarked to anyone who commented on
the benefits of country living that it wouldn't be nearly
so perfect if they didn't have Frank for a neighbor. He
recounted how faithfully Frank would discharge any responsibility of caring for their assorted animals when they
went away on vacation; how Frank would "look out" for
any strangers; how diligently Frank would make sure he

never forgot one of their children's birthdays. The list of kindnesses went on and on.

Now, the kindnesses need to be reversed, Joe thought reflectively. Instead of Frank always on the lookout for us, we need to take the initiative and be sure we are anticipating what he needs. Joe felt sort of overwhelmed by the whole prospect of squeezing in the time it would require to walk over to Frank's house several times a week and take a quick look-see to subtly evaluate how his elderly neighbor was faring, let alone work in the time needed to get Frank's chores done in addition to his own. It didn't take that long, not in hours and minutes, but still Joe recognized that Frank wasn't getting any younger, and he was giving off more and more hints of being unable to handle even minor household repairs and maintenance. Tasks that used to take Frank an hour or so to complete now took almost a full day.

Thinking about the best way to offer some practical assistance, Joe came up with a plan. Joe would mention to Frank that they were trying to find ways for his kids to start serving in the neighborhood (all true). What better way than to engage the whole family in offering to do some simple yard work or even some weekly deep cleaning that Frank couldn't manage anymore? From Joe's perspective, it was a win-win scenario.

Frank would be far more likely to accept this kind of help because it involved the kids, and in a roundabout fashion, the kids would benefit from learning to serve others in need early on in their lives. Joe felt a burden lift off his shoulders. Maybe with all of them pitching in together, Joe and his family could become an integral part of the long-term plan to keep Frank living in his own home for much longer. Always neighbors, thought Joe. But now, we'll just have to remember that we'll be the ones looking out for Frank instead of him looking out for us. *Things really do come full circle eventually*, Joe reflected, *and it's all good.* Although he was a little hesitant to bring up offering help to Frank, Joe was amazed by Frank's grateful response to his gesture, and it did his heart good.

Given the fact that life is always in motion, we would all fare better if we kept our personal expectations of people and relationships (and everything else in between) moving fluidly as well. When Joe first recognized he had been taking for granted that Frank would always be around to help his family, he slowly came around to thinking about specific ways where he and his family could move into the role that Frank had so lovingly taken on years before. Instead of assuming Frank could continue at the same pace, Joe realized that it would most likely have to be he who initiated changes in their relational responsibilities. Frank wasn't going to be the one who backed off from offering his assistance. It would have to be Joe who took the lead firmly but kindly.

Once Joe understood that the balance of his relationship with his neighbor had to shift, Joe rightly started brainstorming practical ways to lighten Frank's daily load. For sure, the first few times that Joe and his kids started taking on Frank's chores, it felt a little awkward and uncomfortable for everyone. But practice makes perfect, and it wasn't long before everyone got into the new routine with lots of gusto and goodwill.

Joe soon realized that his biggest obstacle wasn't the fact that Frank was aging; it was that he needed to adjust his former expectations. When something in our life that has been running smoothly alters, we feel the bump of change deeply. It is unsettling. It is uncomfortable. It puts us out of ease. We suddenly realize that what once worked is now broken—which begs the question of what we can do to repair the situation.

Perhaps like Joe, you're discovering some areas of your life that are shifting and shaking, and you feel uncertain about what's coming next. Don't allow fear to stop you from boldly entering into situations that require some reconsideration and possible revisiting. Do look for positive solutions to creating safe spaces for your loved ones, given their ever-declining skills and abilities. Do it for their peace of mind—and yours.

Take-away Action Thought

When life suddenly shifts and I feel shaken and surprised by the change, I will draw near to God until the ground settles once again—depending on him to help me figure out new ways of dealing with issues as they present themselves.

My Heart's Cry to You, O Lord

I want to give you thanks for the faithfulness of my friend all these years. You truly do set us to live in specific places for specific purposes. This alone is a marvelous truth I cannot fully grasp. What I do know is that the time has come for a genuine role reversal in my relationship with my loved one. Help me to quickly anticipate my friend's needs before he has to come to me for help. Make me sensitive to his feelings and show me kind ways to deflect his growing inability to handle his responsibilities by enthusiastically offering my help with your good grace. Give me your wisdom to understand what a great gift it is to have the physical, mental, emotional, and spiritual resources to help someone who has always been there for me. Amen.

Chapter 9

Learning to Let Go of the Past

Though my father and mother forsake me,
the LORD will receive me.

Psalm 27:10

*The strength of vulnerability is a curious mixture of
discovering your heart and sharing your real self, as
best you can, with the people God has put in your life.*

Paula Rinehart

Kelsey's heart beat a tad faster driving home from work as she anticipated the few minutes of privacy she would enjoy before heading over to her mother's house to check in on her. It had been nine months since her mother's collapse, and once Kelsey's mother had been released from the hospital after an intense two weeks of extensive testing, she had insisted on returning to her own home to live by herself. It hadn't mattered that the doctor strongly advised against it. It hadn't made a whit of difference that Kelsey and her out-of-state brothers suggested a live-in companion. Kelsey's mother did what she'd always done: she did it her way.

Sadly, "her way" was often in opposition to good sense, logical thinking, and frequently the exact opposite of what her family advised her to consider. Kelsey, being the only sibling who lived in town with her mother, felt the brunt of the repercussions from her mother's bad choices. From being reminded that her mother "never did understand her even when she was a child . . ." to having her current decisions berated, Kelsey continually felt pummeled by her mother's critical words and spirit.

But what to do? Kelsey had seen this day coming for quite some time. She knew eventually her mother would need some sort of live-in help to continue on safely in her own home. Yet every time Kelsey broached the topic of hiring professional nursing care and home-care assistance, her mother outright refused to hear of it. Next, Kelsey knew her mother's fallback plan would be to reluctantly tell Kelsey to come live with her. Kelsey would soundly remind her mother that they'd already been there, done that, and it hadn't worked. Kelsey still winced when recalling the year she moved in at her mother's request, and how within weeks her mother decided she didn't have enough privacy. Kelsey tried to reason with her mother. They even set up house rules, and Kelsey adhered to every single one of her mother's specific ways, including how to load and unload the dishwasher. Nothing, absolutely nothing, pleased her mother. Never again, Kelsey thought.

Even harder was the honest truth that, try as she might, Kelsey would never be what her mother wanted her to become. Kelsey's pain of rejection stemmed back to her early days of childhood when her mother's stinging words would wound Kelsey for days on end. How Kelsey had longed for a few words of praise, a hug, or even a smile of affirmation. Instead, her mother was more like a drill sergeant who demanded perfection from everyone in the house.

I should have moved away like my brothers did, Kelsey thought wryly. *But I didn't. I'm here and I'm here to stay. So, putting my emotions aside, I need to decide how to best love and care for Mom.* Kelsey prayed that God would give her the wisdom she needed to anticipate her mother's needs, fulfill them, and then step back from the situation's ongoing volatile emotional minefield. Kelsey realized her mother would very likely die the same embittered, critical woman she was today. But that dismal fact wouldn't stop Kelsey from continuing to love her mother, difficult as she was, with good grace and purposeful intention.

Unfortunately, Kelsey's prediction proved correct. Her mother did eventually pass away as the same unhappy, embittered woman she had been her entire life. Kelsey, though, slowly learned to separate herself from her mother's critical words and caustic spirit.

As Kelsey discovered early on, there are many men and women today who are doing their level best to take good care of their aging parents. Instead of receiving a heartfelt thank-you, or even a simple smile of gratitude for good deeds done on their behalf, some adult children find themselves in a situation similar to Kelsey's. There is no positive response one might reasonably expect from lovingly serving and caring for another's needs. Rather, like Kelsey, some elderly parents exhibit more hostility the older they get. As old age takes hold, many personality traits become more pronounced. Social filters seem to disappear, and older parents say what they think despite the fallout on the listener.

Kelsey wisely realized that given her mother's lifelong bent for being a critical and negative person, she probably wouldn't change much before she passed away. Again, what to do? Kelsey spent some time reflecting on her life as a child, then as a teen, and now as an adult in relation to her mother. After having endured a painful childhood, Kelsey now understood that her mother's own wounds had played a large part in how she had parented Kelsey and her brothers. Was it right? Not in the least. But it may have been the best she had to offer them.

As an adult, Kelsey also recognized that her mother's ongoing bitterness toward past life losses had poisoned her life today. Not wanting a repeat performance in her own life, Kelsey worked hard to forgive others when she was wronged—and she included her mother's poor behavior and ill-chosen remarks in that habit of forgiveness as well. While it's never easy to love the unloving, there is a strong biblical principle that comes into play when we determine to overcome evil with good. When we opt to love those who don't have a clue about how to love us, we take God at his word and can expect his strengthening grace to uphold us. As we continue to invest ourselves in these vital family relationships, we might very well see God do something quite unexpected and exceptional before the last conversation is spoken.

Take-away Action Thought

God will give me the strength, the wisdom, and the grace to love my parents, no matter how unlovingly they respond to me. I need him to help me stop taking their ill-worded comments to heart by reminding me that they endured much unhappiness throughout their own childhoods.

My Heart's Cry to You, O Lord

Please help me to keep my eyes trained on you as I seek to honor my parents, respect them, and meet their needs. You know how difficult the past has been for me to work through—the unkindness, the harsh words, even the neglect. But you were there for me when my parents were not. Help me to focus on overcoming evil with good, and by your enabling strength I will learn how to love more deeply, more sacrificially, than ever before. Enable me to treat my parents as I would hope to be treated. Amen.

Chapter 10

Time Equals Love

Do nothing out of selfish ambition or vain
conceit. Rather, in humility value others above
yourselves, not looking to your own interests but
each of you to the interests of the others.

Philippians 2:3–4

When you start taking charge of your life, a
seemingly insignificant but responsible action
can lead to a significant outcome.
Richard L. Ganz

Matt was stressed out. He was feeling the pressure at
work to give more time, more energy, more of himself to his
job. Matt was feeling pressure from his wife and kids too.
They just wanted him home more. Matt was also feeling
pressure from himself—every time he took a few moments
to reflect upon the sad truth that he'd developed the same
work habits as his father so many years before. Matt's "absent" father is how he always referred to him.

Matt's father was feeling stressed too, and a life full of
regrets haunted his daily thoughts—though he couldn't
quite figure out when the obsession to succeed vocationally

had taken precedence over everything and everyone in his life. Matt could have told him. Matt's sister remembered growing up without a father around too, and it was a subject she and Matt revisited from time to time. As a widower, Matt's father now had a lot of hours each day to reflect upon his life, his choices, and his priorities. He realized he hadn't been around enough to be the father he'd hoped he would be when his family was young and starting out. But then the push to advance came once and then a second time and a third. Finally, he stopped counting. He never said no to advancement, not once. After all, more money meant fewer worries.

Too late Matt's father realized that his children had grown up and moved away before he had really gotten to know either of them. Of course, his wife had been the link between them all. She stayed the course, kept the family together, and then she died. Since then, his regret over his long absences had loomed larger every day. But Matt's father didn't know how to reconnect with Matt and his sister. He didn't have a clue. *Time*, thought Matt's father, *I wish I had had more time.*

Ironically, Matt was thinking along the same lines. Matt remembered the ups and downs of his childhood with a father who was never there, and he didn't want his children feeling the same loss he had experienced. Matt also recognized he had been harboring some quiet resentment toward his father for a while now. Matt wasn't about to waste the little bit of free time he did have on the man who had had no time for him. No way.

And yet, something had been needling Matt recently. He couldn't deny the fact that he was growing into the same type of man his father had been. Ouch. Was it too late? Was there still a chance they could find a way to reconnect as father and son? Matt realized he wanted to try. He also recognized that getting to know his father would mean saying no to other things in his life. It might take some time to find the time, but Matt knew a few small changes he could begin making this week even to pare back: reinvesting in his family, spending more time with them and his father—it was a good plan. A right decision. A timely one.

One of the great ironies of life is that we often get to a place where we better understand why the people in our lives made the choices they made because we've become, in part, just like them. Oh sure, we can swear we'll never be like (fill in the blank), but unless we keep our accounts clean and live full of forgiveness toward those who have failed us, we often mirror the very people we harbor anger against.

Matt would never have guessed that he would in any way, shape, or form take on the same work ethic as his father had—but he did. It wasn't until after Matt found himself into a similar fix that he began to realize he had made the same poor choices as his father. Likewise, it took Matt's father enduring his wife's passing and his subsequent loneliness to figure out how he had failed as a younger man.

Both men, however, now have the opportunity for a relationship re-do. Thankfully, in this case, it wasn't too late to set things right by asking for forgiveness, and then make amends by forging a better and different way through life.

Like so many adult children who have uneasy relationships with their elderly parents, it's almost too easy to see the parents' errors while failing to dig deeper into the "why" of those choices. Only when we intentionally begin to place others' welfare above our own can we hope to mend those broken fences with kindness and understanding. Making time for others truly does equal love.

Take-away Action Thought

I will intentionally set aside specific
times this week to spend with my family,
my parents, and my friends. I will also
choose to put aside any feelings I still
have of being neglected as a child.

My Heart's Cry to You, O Lord

Today, Lord, help me make wise choices regarding how I choose to spend these next hours. I know I struggle against a myriad of demands that come to me every single day. I therefore need your fresh perspective on work, rest, leisure, and time spent with family. Give me the discipline to say no to too many opportunities, and give me a mind of peace to trust you to guide my thoughts and actions. Show me how to rebuild those relationships that have broken down, and give me the good sense to always put others' welfare above my own. Amen.

Chapter 11

Challenging the Widowed Parent to Keep Living

Rejoice always, pray continually, give
thanks in all circumstances; for this is
God's will for you in Christ Jesus.
1 Thessalonians 5:16–18

*Depressed people, like all of us, are aware of kindness
and love that is willing to sacrifice. Love always
leaves its mark. As a result, depressed people who
do best are cushioned by persevering love.*
Edward Welch

We were standing in the church hallway after Sunday
services when my good friend Jesse walked up to ask me a
question. As we chatted, I was so distracted by the way her
mother shadowed her that I could hardly concentrate on
what Jesse was asking me. Only later when we were alone
did I have the opportunity to inquire about her mother's
health (physical, emotional, and spiritual). What Jesse
shared with me made me so sad. So very, very sad.

Two years ago, Jesse and her husband added a beautiful
in-laws' apartment to their home. I had a chance to tour it

right after they completed the project, and it was gorgeous. I thought how grateful Jesse's parents would be to live in such lovely quarters while also being so close to their family. Not long after they moved in, Jesse's father became sick and passed away before they'd even spent a full year in their new home.

After the grief subsided, Jesse made it her mission to keep her mother occupied with family goings-on, church functions, senior center classes, and by taking her along for the ride whenever she ran errands. Jesse tried every single day to get her mother out of the house. To no avail. The only place her mother would agree to go to was Sunday church services. Sigh.

Even then, Jesse hardly had a moment to herself because her mother literally shadowed her every move. No matter who Jesse talked with, her mother stood right behind her. No matter how Jesse tried to engage her mother with others in conversation, her mother stood silent. No matter what. Nothing seemed to draw Jesse's mother out of her morose state of mind.

After a while, Jesse herself grew overwhelmed by the prospect of constantly attempting to bring new life into her mother's stalled one. The entire family tried their best to get Grandma out and about and interested in old hobbies, lifelong friends, and church activities. It felt like they were trudging up a mountain with no end in sight. Before her father had passed away, Jesse's mother was the life of the party. She was social, engaging, intelligent, and highly active. Now, she had turned almost silent, depressed, uninterested, and paralyzed by grief.

Jesse still doesn't know if her mother will ever turn a corner emotionally before she, too, passes away. Jesse, for her part, is determined to keep encouraging her mother to find new ways to live again. Jesse won't give up—she understands that perseverance is essential, and she won't quit on her mother. Loving her through her grief is a worthy goal. Even when Jesse doesn't always believe she is getting through, she is, because we know that love always leaves its mark.

I would venture to say that every person alive suffers tough seasons when they feel like life and its accompanying trials just aren't worth the effort. But we get through to the other side, we look back, and we realize how much those tough times have forced us to mature and grow in character and become, well, tougher. Whether the challenges present themselves to us when we are age eight, eighteen, thirty-eight, or eighty, as long as we have breath in our bodies, God has a plan for us.

Certainly, as we age those plans change right along with our changing minds and bodies. Still, God is watching over our lives, and he expects each of us to continue using the gifts he has given us. God never puts an end date on offering our lives as a living sacrifice to him, as stated in Romans 12. Sadly, many who are in the retirement age bracket feel as though they've done their time, given their service, and are deserving of a full-time rest. Not so.

Like Jesse, not only will we find ourselves facing adjustments as we age, but we'll probably be required to encourage our aging parents to keep living once grief and loss take a toll. Jesse learned through experience that her mother didn't want to live anymore. But does Jesse give up? Never. She keeps on plugging along, daily nudging her mother to choose wisely by doing the same. May each of us exhibit the same stamina and stick-to-it-iveness that Jesse demonstrates daily as she continues to offer positive life choices to her mother.

Take-away Action Thought

I refuse to grow angry, discouraged, or depressed even though my aging parents may choose sad responses to life's losses. Instead, I will keep working hard to bring them new opportunities to get out and involved, and I will model by example how I hope they will decide to spend their final years.

My Heart's Cry to You, O Lord

Help me, Father, to consistently offer opportunities to my aging parents, even when they repeatedly refuse me. Help me to be sensitive to the grief they may be experiencing and try not to rush them through it. When I observe them in the mires of discouragement and depression, give me words to encourage, hope to inspire, and love to comfort. Draw near, Lord, to us all, and help us stay in tune with your Holy Spirit as you nudge us into serving others by serving you. Amen.

Chapter 12

Reminding Parents of the Positive Aspects of Their Life

Yet the LORD longs to be gracious to you;
therefore he will rise up to show you
compassion.
For the LORD is a God of justice.
Blessed are all who wait for him!

Isaiah 30:18

The sea, dry land, winter cold, summer heat,
morning light, evening shade are full of thee,
and thou givest me them richly to enjoy.

Arthur Bennett

Deb's mother's name was Nancy—and all through her life, folks teasingly called her "Negative Nancy." Deb, of course, never actually called her mother by that true but not-so-nice nickname, but she sure thought it. Every day on her way home from work, Deb called her mother and they talked—or rather, her mother talked and Deb tried to get a word in edgewise. Deb had discovered over the years that living in a state distant from her mother was a good thing. She had watched her brothers take the brunt of her mother's sharp tongue, and her constant complaining had worn them down.

While Deb didn't see her mother much, she had privately committed to calling her Monday through Friday en route home from work. This promise was one of the most trying twenty minutes of Deb's day. She often thought to herself that facing a hundred hormonal teens would have been easier than making the daily attempt to encourage her mother to see the bright side of life. Knowing her mother's penchant for negativity, Deb often searched for upbeat greeting cards, worship music, and Scriptures that promised God's care to those he loved.

Rarely did Deb ever see any evidence of a glimmer of gratitude from her mother—which is one reason why Deb wisely talked to her mother only on the way home from work, thus having an endpoint for the conversation. Deb repeatedly mentioned how consistently her brothers showed up every week to mow her mother's grass, put out the trash cans, shop for her groceries, and even take her out for dinner—to which her mother, being Negative Nancy, would always find fault with some aspect of their care. Deb honestly didn't know how her brothers stood it. She struggled just with phone calls. So, in addition to her daily calls to her mother, Deb sent up daily prayers for her brothers.

It's been said before but it bears repeating again: Any area we have not dealt with in our youth or in midlife will come out in extremes as we age. Sure, our folks may chronologically be considered mature, but that does not mean they are mature emotionally. Individuals who have harbored bitter, angry, resentful attitudes during their lives will end up as bitter, angry, resentful older adults without the normal social filters people have when they are younger.

Of course, some bad behavior may be caused by a physical illness such as dementia, a urinary tract infection, or some other medical condition, perhaps due to a change in medications. At times, adult children will feel as if they are trying to master a complex puzzle with a few of the pieces missing. At other times, a simple change in a prescription may bring a cure. Certainly, as Deb experienced with her mother, any lifelong habit that has characterized a personality will be hardest to deal with, and healthy parameters must be set up by the caregiving adult children. Every situation will be a subjective one, and only those involved will know how much they can do and how to best implement their care.

In Deb's case, her brothers couldn't believe that Deb took the time every day to call their mother—they couldn't do it. On the other hand, Deb found it more incredible that her brothers continued doing all of their mother's chores when she complained incessantly about how they were done. For Deb's family, the plan they had going was working. It wasn't perfect. It certainly wasn't easy. But for now, it was the best they could do in an unfortunate circumstance with their ungrateful mother.

Take-away Action Thought

When my parent's bad behavior takes over, I will try to discover where the root of the problem lies and then correct it—or make peace with it. I will also purpose to pray more diligently for my parent and for those serving her.

My Heart's Cry to You, O Lord

It is a wonder to me that none of us children have taken on our parents' negativity. Certainly, you must have been protecting us when we were growing up. All I know is that none of us ever wanted to end up like our folks—those whose lives were governed by complaints and resentment. It surely clouded much of our childhood, and yet you brought in the light through others who showed us a better way to live. I will continue to challenge my folks to adopt a thankful heart to you, Lord. I will not stop praying that they discover you and your gift of eternal life as the greatest treasure of all. Amen.

Chapter 13

Focusing on the Eternal When the Temporal Feels Too Painful

Therefore, there is now no condemnation for
those who are in Christ Jesus, because through
Christ Jesus the law of the Spirit who gives life
has set you free from the law of sin and death.

Romans 8:1–2

*I triumph now in thy promises as I
shall do in their performance.*

Arthur Bennett

Guilt. Guilt. Guilt. That's what Mandy felt every single day after any interaction with her parents. Mandy never spent enough time with them. Mandy didn't care enough about them. Mandy didn't do enough for them. The litany of accusations (from her parents) and the self-recriminations (from her own thoughts) preyed on her day and night. Was it any wonder she loved to lose herself in a good book or movie? Mandy truly felt emotional relief only when she was actively thinking about something or someone other than her mother and father.

This whole guilt "trip" started when Mandy was only a child. As she recalled it to me, she would walk over two streets a couple of times a week during the summer months to visit her grandparents while her folks were at work. Mandy remembers loving her grandparents and they loved her—maybe too much? Every time she visited, Mandy nursed a stomachache while dreading what she knew would happen when she told her grandparents it was time to leave. Her grandfather would try to convince her to play one more game of checkers, and her grandmother would scurry to the kitchen in search of an enticing snack to prolong the visit. This lingering memory Mandy had of disappointing her grandparents with every goodbye still haunted her as an adult.

With her grandparents now deceased some twenty-plus years, Mandy thought those childhood aches and pains would have long ago disappeared. Wrong. Today, she feels the same roiling sense of anxiety take residence deep inside of her every time the caller ID on her phone says it's her parents, her inbox has an e-mail from her folks, or she checks her daily planner and an upcoming appointment reminds her of an approaching visit. Mandy's mother and father have somehow (consciously or unconsciously) taken on the same habit her grandparents had all those years ago. They make Mandy feel guilty when she needs to hang up after a phone chat, when she doesn't reply to an e-mail with enough detail to suit them, and when she gets up to leave after a visit.

Mandy has tried to figure out why she allows her parents' unrealistic expectations to jade their relationship. She doesn't allow it with any other relationship at work or with friends. Puzzled and almost depressed, Mandy decided to spend some time with the Lord praying, asking for insight, begging for wisdom, and simply allowing God's unconditional love to wash over her and refresh her. Mandy turned off her phone. She closed her inbox. She cleared her calendar for the weekend. She did the wisest thing possible—she unplugged from the source of frustration to better understand how to handle it in the future.

After that happily quiet weekend, Mandy did gain some important insights about herself and her parents. She realized she couldn't change her parents or lower their expectations, but she could change hers. No longer would she live in hopeful expectation that her mother and father would ever be satisfied. No longer would she expect them to be reasonable. Most important, Mandy realized she'd spent far too much time and energy trying to please people who would not be pleased no matter what she did. For the first time in years, Mandy felt free from the inside out.

Sometimes (a lot of times?), today's relationships with our parents are riddled with unrealistic expectations and guilt—lots and lots of guilt. It's not that adult children by and large aren't stepping up and serving their aging parents. Most are. I think, rather, it's simply that some older adults have forgotten how hard they worked to keep hearth and home together when they were younger. Aging parents sometimes (a lot of times?) genuinely don't remember how they got up early, worked all day, came home, and spent the evening working more at home.

But knowing this doesn't make it any easier to handle living with the unkind comments, the underhanded subtle criticisms, or the outright bold rude remarks. Most older people (or, for that matter, any people) will not change unless the Lord does a magnificent work in their (and our) lives. But how many of our parents are willing to do the hard work it takes to overhaul their attitudes, actions, and lives? Not many, I'm guessing.

Just as Mandy eventually came to accept that her parents weren't changing, she also had to change the way she handled their ill-motivated remarks. Mandy had to come to peace with the fact that in this life relationships aren't always what we hoped, prayed, and dreamed they would become. So, like Mandy, we too have to temper our expectations of the aging folks in our lives, commit our hopes for relational peace, and set our sights on eternity—where we know we will not be disappointed.

Take-away Action Thought

When feelings of false guilt rise up in me
and I feel overwhelmed by sadness, I will
turn to Scripture and linger over the passages
that speak of God's unconditional love
for me. No longer will I take on guilt for
something I have not done (or left undone).

My Heart's Cry to You, O Lord

Help me to speak your truth into my heart. I need your strong counsel of truth to cling to day and night. I'm often left feeling shamed by my family when I don't meet their expectations. This isn't something I want to keep experiencing day in and day out. You know, Lord, that I try my best to meet my parents' needs, but it is never enough. I've always dreamed of having a close relationship with my folks, but I'm realizing it may never come to be. Instead of living with this false guilt, help me to serve faithfully and keep my eyes on eternity. My hope is in you alone, Lord. Amen.

Chapter 14

Dealing with a Difficult Childhood

Do not be overcome by evil, but overcome evil with good.
Romans 12:21

*Good is so much more powerful than evil
that, by comparison, evil is but a pop gun.
Good, in contrast, is a nuclear weapon.*

Jay Adams

Troy and Kim, married for over twenty-five years, have had their share of ups and downs through the years. Kim's father was (and is) a sick man. From childhood on, Kim recalled either feeling terrified of her father's anger or, in contrast, feeling like he was the best and funniest man on the planet. The problem was that Kim and her siblings never knew which man was going to walk through the front door each evening. Case in fact: one cold winter evening, Kim's father flew into such a rage that he actually tore the front door off its hinges and threw it into the snow.

Understandably, Kim and Troy were hesitant to take in her father after a debilitating stroke left him unable to live alone any longer. Troy couldn't believe that after her horrific childhood (the scars of which still cause Kim panic attacks today) she would even toy with the idea of housing her father. Kim completely understood Troy's hesitation, but she believed with all her heart that she had recovered from her father's violent history and wanted to make the attempt to care for him in his final years.

Both Kim and Troy offered up sound reasons for their opposing stances on this issue. Each evening, they'd approach the topic again and try their best to see the other's point of view. But it wasn't happening. Troy felt protective of his wife, and rightly so. Kim felt that God had done a significant work of healing in her heart, and she wanted to put into practice Romans 12:21, which says, "Overcome evil with good."

From where I sat, I saw both of their perspectives and told them I would pray. Either Kim's father would move in and all would go smoothly (the stroke had in fact mellowed him thus far), or Kim would find herself reliving the nightmare of her childhood once again. As it stands today, until Kim and Troy can come to an agreement, they have opted to wait. Wait and pray. Sounds like a plan to me.

❧

The scenario described above is more common than I realized before I began asking friends, family, and acquaintances to share their childhood stories about their relationship with their parents. Sadly, a number of households from my era had much pain, suffering, and untold anger in them. When I reflect upon Kim's childhood, I feel such sadness for her and her father. I knew her father personally, and I can remember visiting her home when I was a teenager and how her father was the life of the party. It was marvelous! Then there were those other visits when I attempted to say hello to Kim's father, and he would look right through me. That . . . wasn't so great.

Wisely, after Kim and Troy married, they realized (as we all do) that we are in large part products of our childhood family unit. For good. For bad. We become in part the people we observed while we were growing up. Kim knew instinctively that the relationship she had with her father wasn't a healthy one, and so she sought biblical counseling. Therein lies the main reason Kim believes she was able to look into her past and see it for what it was. She now understands that her father's anger was because *he* had a problem, not because *she* did something wrong.

Like so many adults who grew up in abusive homes, Kim still fights the lies that sometimes try to consume her thoughts. Wisely, she has learned to combat these destructive thoughts with pure, powerful Bible verses that annihilate wrong thinking.

Kim is much freer from her past than ever before. With continued right thinking, Kim knows that no matter how unhealthy her past was, today and tomorrow shine bright with future hope because of Christ.

Take-away Action Thought

When I feel the pain of my past rear its ugly head to steal today's peace, I will turn to God's word and speak his truth aloud. I will daily spend time in the Bible meditating on those Scriptures that speak of God's unconditional love for me.

My Heart's Cry to You, O Lord

Father, I am continually wavering between feeling stuck in my painful past and experiencing true freedom today. There is nothing more I desire on earth than to forget my painful childhood. But I cannot do so. Help me instead to see the past through your lens of forgiveness and restoration. I know you can bring permanent healing to my heart and mind. Better yet, I know you can restore all those lost years of suffering because your word promises this. Help me to sink deeply into the words that speak healing to me as I find them in your promises. Change me, Lord, from the inside out, from a fearful, frightened child to a Christ-empowered, grace-filled, Spirit-led person of God. Amen.

Chapter 15

Seeing Older Parents through the Lens of Grace

The heart is deceitful above all things
and beyond cure.
Who can understand it?
Jeremiah 17:9

*Being a Christian does not mean that we are free
of spiritual blindness or the potential for self-
deception. As long as there is indwelling sin,
spiritual blindness and self-deception will exist.*
Paul David Tripp

Two friends of ours (who shall remain nameless) were having breakfast with my husband and me some time ago when I inquired about the health of their parents. Without a pause, the husband replied, "Still as mean as snakes—both of them." His wife, gentle soul that she is, shook her head and then tried explaining the rest of the story. "His folks have been hounding us day and night for months now about the littlest issues. They call about the smallest problems and expect us to drop everything, drive over, listen to their complaints, fix whatever's broken, and then they complain some more. That part," she continued, "we can deal with. It's the backstabbing and lies they tell about us to the rest of the family that is driving us both crazy."

Having known this couple for over twenty years, we knew better than to believe any negative talk about either of them. As we sat eating our breakfast, however, it became clear our friends were having a hard time handling all the nastiness coming from their parents. "Maybe the most painful slap on the face," she continued, "is when we take them out to a restaurant, and they gush sweetness at everyone they meet. Even the waitresses look at us and say things like, 'You're so lucky to have such wonderful parents. They're just the cutest couple ever.' Which of course makes us feel like choking back a truthful reply. Instead, we weakly smile."

Oh boy. My husband and I didn't know what to say. Or do. It's tough enough when it's a stranger or an acquaintance treating you one way to your face and another behind your back. But when it's your parents, the stakes run much higher. The pain etched on their faces spoke of the toll this situation was taking on both of our friends. Long after that breakfast was over, we continued to discuss how we might handle such a scenario. We honestly weren't sure how we would deal with something like this—and hoped we would never have to find out.

One snatch of that conversation still lingers with me today. I keep remembering the wife saying, "They really believe their lives honor the Lord. But how can they deceive themselves like this? Can't they see how their words are hurtful, not to mention untrue?" Good question. I'm reminded of the passage in Jeremiah that states that the heart is deceitful above all things. Could it be that our friends' folks are simply blinded by their own sin?

The sad scenario described above is a strong case for having an accountability partner or partners set up in our lives. There's not a soul alive who doesn't need a person (or many) who will tell them the hard truth about sin in their lives. There's not a soul alive who won't benefit in the here and now (as well as eternity) by having someone who will direct them back to God and God's standard of living biblically toward others.

Sadly, accountability has gone out of favor in our fast-paced, driven society where we live increasingly independent lives with few friends or family members who will reprove us when we need correction. As Paul Tripp states above, "As long as there is indwelling sin, spiritual blindness and self-deception will exist." If only our friends' parents had a few contemporaries who were willing to speak up and help redirect their hurtful conversation. If only the other adult children in the family would take the initiative to gently challenge their folks' untruths when they berated others. If only someone would take God seriously when he said we are all responsible for confronting sin when we see it, in the hopes of restoring those who have lost their way. Let this sad scenario be a poignant warning: None of us is immune to faulty thinking, sinful speech, or a heart governed by ingratitude. But for the grace of God, go I.

Take-away Action Thought

When I hear someone gossip or speak an untruth about another person, I will remove myself from the conversation or gently challenge the one who is talking. Likewise, I will ask my closest friends to keep me accountable as to how I speak about others.

My Heart's Cry to You, O Lord

Father, in my heart of hearts, I love my parents but I do not love the way they talk. From listening to the words that come out of their mouths, anyone would believe they are mistreated, neglected, and abandoned by their family, by us. Yet I know this is not true. Show me creative ways to break through their faulty misconceptions. Help me have the courage to challenge them when they speak untruths in a way that is loving and respectful. Give me your compassion for them, while simultaneously steering them back to what you teach us about the weight of our words. I need your grace to forgive their hard words and your strength to continue loving them, even if they choose not to change. Amen.

Chapter 16

Learning to Listen Well, Again and Again

A gentle answer turns away wrath,
but a harsh word stirs up anger.

Proverbs 15:1

*All day long the choice will be before us in a
thousand ways. It will mean a constant yielding
to those around us, for our yieldedness to God
is measured by our yieldedness to man.*

Roy Hession

Several years ago I sat with a terrific woman over lunch, and somehow we ventured onto the topic of her elderly mother. My friend Cindy is an only child, and so it is her responsibility to see to her mother's care. Right now, that means stopping over after work a few times a week to drop off groceries or medicines. Cindy's mother relies on a senior service to drive her to her medical appointments during the day. All in all, Cindy knows she is fortunate that her mother doesn't yet require more in-house care.

And yet, isn't there always something that causes us anxiety and/or internal upset? For Cindy, it was her mother's incessant need to retell her personal history. Over the past few years, Cindy has retold me (and I never forget the dilemma she is in) how her mother is bent on telling and retelling the same stories from her earlier years again and again and again. It wasn't so bad the first ten times or so—but after fifty-plus retellings of the same old story, it gets tiring! Stifling a laugh, Cindy freely admits (as do I) that now that we're in our mid-fifties, we forget things too.

Cindy shared with me that it isn't simply that she is growing weary of her mother repeating herself time and again; it's how, with the frequent retellings, somehow her mother is increasingly revising the stories, becoming the shining star in each memory. "I feel like my mom is not only forgetting—she is becoming a liar! And I hate that I feel this way about my mom." Cindy and I discussed some gentle ways she might consider approaching her mother the next time she starts her habitual retelling.

Cindy wants to love and honor her mother no matter what changes take place in her personality. Still, the way it's heading, Cindy is beginning to dread her visits more and more. Hopefully, Cindy's new plan of attack will work as she tries new and different ways to kindly steer the conversation into new arenas. All in all, Cindy is doing a wonderful job meeting the needs of her mother and handling the changes with good grace. Still, like all of us, Cindy needs a daily refreshing from God's word to remind her that regardless of how she feels, a gentle answer is the way to go.

It is so easy to say we are ready for whatever God has planned for us—until he chooses a particular task to do or person to serve that we don't want to engage in or with. Right? I love the quote above from Roy Hession's book, *Calvary Road*, where he cuts directly to the heart of the matter when he says that the way in which we lay down our rights in favor of another's rights is the proportion to which we honestly submit to God himself. Ouch.

I can so relate to Cindy's predicament. I want to do what is right by those in my family (and among my friends) and yet, at times, what is required of me "feels" like too much. I'm too busy. I'm too tired. I'm too involved. I'm too . . . whatever. When I read Hession's quote, I'm reminded that as a Christ follower I have been commanded to present myself as a gift offering to the Lord for his use (Romans 12). Therefore, how he chooses to use me (my gifts, talents, time, and resources) are truly inconsequential. My availability and my willingness to serve is what matters.

Like Cindy, there will come a day when I'll be called upon to serve (again) in ways not of my own choosing. I'll be spending my hours perhaps listening to the same stories retold a hundred times (with perhaps a hundred different twists). I'll be devoting my energy to making sure someone else is cared for and comfortable.

Above all, I purpose (as does my friend Cindy) to complete every act of service by the grace of God, and by extending gentleness, kindness, and mercy. Lots and lots of mercy.

Take-away Action Thought

Whenever I begin to feel impatient and upset during conversations with someone I'm called to serve, I will thank the good Lord for the soundness of mind I still have and will extend mercy in abundance. Even when I begin to feel impatient with my loved one's conversation, I will purposely sit back and give her all the attention she needs.

My Heart's Cry to You, O Lord

Father, help me to remember that you have designed our beginnings and our endings. You have created these bodies that grow old and eventually wear out. Help me to show kindness, patience, gentleness, and loads of mercy—for I know that one day I'll be in need of this same care. In the meantime, guide my words to bring encouragement and love. Grant me an abundance of generous goodwill toward everyone who listens to me. Above all, help me realize that even the smallest act of kindness extended toward another is never wasted, never squandered, when done in your name. Amen.

Chapter 17

Theirs, Mine, and Ours

Let us therefore make every effort to do what
leads to peace and to mutual edification.

Romans 14:19

*You may feel your choices have been reduced to whether
you want Jell-O or a window opened or an extra
blanket. On the contrary, your choice of whether you
will trust God and worship him today reverberates
throughout the universe, honoring or dishonoring
your God. It also has enormous implications for the
eternal rewards God promises us in the next life.*

Randy Alcorn

Alison found herself in the place no one wants to be:
right in the middle of a dispute between her mother and
stepfather and his children. When her mother remarried
years earlier, Alison took to her new stepfather right away.
Alison's birth father had never been in the picture, so to her
mind, Alison's stepfather was her father. Unlike Alison, her
two step-siblings did not feel like Alison's mother was their
"real" mother, even though, like Alison, their birth mother
had abandoned them when they were in elementary school.

As Alison grew up, turmoil in the way of petty bickering and small jealousies was the norm in their home. She never quite understood where her step-siblings got all their anger, or why they kept refueling it with minor complaints. Of course, this caused distance between Alison and them. Her step-siblings viewed Alison as counterpart to their number one enemy, Alison's mother.

In Alison's mother's case, this is where the traditional "stepmother" bad rap was proven wrong. Alison's mother loved all three of "her" kids just the same, and there were moments when Alison had hoped her mother would favor her even a little bit—but it never happened. When Alison grew up and moved away from home, she saw less and less of her step-siblings. Then her parents got older, and they started needed more in-house assistance, which Alison was happy to offer.

What Alison didn't realize was that her step-siblings were harboring yet another insult to injury, because they believed Alison was showing up only to help so that their parents would give her a larger share of their inheritance. Ridiculous. That's what Alison told her folks when they warned her about the upcoming firestorm that was brewing. Alison naturally wouldn't let her step-siblings' troublesome comments stop her from doing what was right, so she kept right on showing up and caring for those she loved most in the world.

After a season of relative peace, Alison's folks asked her to become executor of their estate because, in a word, they trusted her. Alison didn't want the job, but she knew it was her parents' wish. On the day they signed the necessary documents, her stepfather pulled her aside and simultaneously thanked her and warned her: "Don't let my kids bully you after we're gone!" "I won't, Dad, I won't." In truth, Alison didn't know what she was dreading most—the passing of her beloved parents or having to contend with the upset she knew was coming from her step-siblings.

The repercussions of broken relationships never cease, even though both parties are doing their best to make different and better choices in their futures. It shouldn't surprise anyone that this truth is often played out most dramatically within the confines of the family unit. Mom and Dad marry, split up, remarry, add a few kids in for good measure, and you have the makings for some potentially volatile happenings.

The truth is it was no one's fault that Alison's step-siblings chose to grow up angry and then stay angry at the world. Their parents did their best with consistent love and care to break down their walls of resentment, but they were not successful—because in truth, the step-siblings didn't want to let go of their anger. Alison, growing up on the sidelines of their continual grievances, tried to stay out of it, but is that possible when you live side by side in one home?

Perhaps the farthest reaching lesson that Alison walked away with was that each individual can choose how to interpret the good, the bad, and the ugly in their lives. How we decide to respond makes all the difference in how well we can walk forward into our future with healing and hope. Alison does have a tough road ahead of her, but she is wise enough to put all her hope and trust in God and his faithful provision—and she continues to lift up her step-siblings to the only One who can heal and restore them.

Take-away Action Thought

When I see a relational storm brewing, I will find my hiding place in God alone. I will also endeavor to plant my feet firmly in the center of his will and refuse to compromise on doing what is right.

My Heart's Cry to You, O Lord

I never asked for this job, Lord, but to make my parents happy I said yes. I wonder if they fully realize how much stress and headache I'm in for after they pass away. Our entire growing up has been darkened by the jealousy and envy of my step-siblings. You know I never wanted that and most of the time I didn't even understand what they were angry about. Help me to be wise in my every interaction with them. Give me the grace I need to respond with kindness, even if they are unkind. I will need your strength day by day to maintain my heart of peace and not become anxious or upset by their words and actions. Remind me to run to you, Jesus, when I am most afraid. Amen.

Chapter 18

Recognizing Your Parents' Personalities May Completely Disappear

But you, God, see the trouble of the afflicted;
you consider their grief and take it in hand.

Psalm 10:14

I am safe because You have given me the one thing
that is the only thing that will ever keep me safe. You.

Paul David Tripp

Beth woke up every morning with a knot in her stomach, and she went to bed every night with the same sinking pit of despair shrouding her final waking thoughts. Ever since my dear friend and her always generous husband made room in their home for Beth's parents, their lives had taken a difficult turn. Beth and Tim had talked long and hard about any potential upsets that might occur once Beth's folks moved into their finished basement (now a beautifully redone in-laws' apartment). They anticipated some bumps in the road as everyone made adjustments. What they hadn't counted on was the unexpected death of Beth's father less than a year after the move.

Beth's father had been a driven, cold, and cantankerous man right until his death at age ninety. Beth's mother had always been the soft-spoken, gentle-hearted companion who never once complained. After her father died, Beth noticed a change in her mother's attitude and behavior. What was once a kindly, caring woman suddenly transformed into a hateful, embittered, and quite frankly, ungrateful stranger. Beth and Tim were (and are) at a loss to explain the dramatic change in her mother's personality.

Could it be grief? Might it be a physical problem? A spiritual one? I've listened to Beth explain this unlikely transformation, and like my friend, I too am clueless. More distressing than the "why" behind the change is the "how do we continue to handle this stranger living among us?" Beth explained that it is hard enough when her mother complains to her and Tim about everything, but lately she has started verbally harassing their two teenage daughters—who now avoid their grandmother's presence.

What to do? Beth has tried sitting down with her mother and talking through her mother's complaints. She has tried family meetings in which the entire clan sits and candidly discusses the problems. Beth and Tim together have taken her mother out to dinner and gently turned the conversation toward possible solutions. Nothing makes any difference. It seems as if every conversation is laced with anger, bitter retorts, and ever-escalating disappointments.

When Beth and I spoke recently, I could see the tension rise in her as she related her growing impatience with how her mother was treating her daughters. Obviously protective of her children's welfare, Beth is trying to find an alternative way to care for her mother. Looking across the table at my friend, I felt for her and was again reminded that there aren't any easy answers for such a deep-seated problem. I often think of Beth and Tim, remembering to pray for God's strength and grace to carry them through each day while supplying them with the wisdom they need for the days to come.

⁕

Our best-laid plans often go awry. We think, we plan, we pray, and then we make a choice we believe is best for everyone concerned. And perhaps it is. However, as much as we attempt to plan well, prepare sufficiently, and pray for smooth sailing, life gets in the way. Our plans fail. Our prayers turn to pleading. Our patience fizzles, and we're left wondering where we went wrong.

Like my friend realized, we can think, plan, and pray, and still unexpected twists in our story (and in our parents') will happen. The challenge then is how to make the best of the worst possible scenario. As my friend came to understand, often there are not simple solutions. She and her husband continue to love and serve her mother, but they understand they are equally responsible for meeting the needs of their daughters. So, whose needs take precedence? Parents? Children? Back and forth like a seesaw, they try to meet everyone's needs every day.

Beth and Tim know that God will direct them eventually. In the meantime, they continue to get up each morning, ask God for the strength to do the right thing, and keep on serving until he shows them a different plan. They are purposing to find their strength and safety in the sure knowledge that they *are* safe in him. They know that God will reveal his best solution to their problems (large and small) at the right moment. Until then, they continue to commit themselves to God's care, trusting that he reigns from on high and is completely aware of the trials they face hourly—because he does reign and is present, aware, and in control. Amen.

Take-away Action Thought

When I feel as if my entire world is coming apart at the seams, I will step out of the fray and silently seek God's presence. I will also remind myself that despite my best intentions my loved one may never show any appreciation or gratefulness for how I have provided for her.

My Heart's Cry to You, O Lord

Father, help me to have the good sense, the common sense, and your heavenly wisdom to know how to handle this touchy situation with my parents. I understand that often our best-laid plans can abruptly change when physical illnesses appear, losses trigger grief, and simple aging causes people to lash out. I want to love my parents in a way that is both comforting to them and brings honor to you, but I frequently fail in this endeavor. Lately, I find myself irritable, worried, and sick to my stomach. I cannot sleep at night. Help me, Lord, to reestablish my inner rest and peace in you. You alone are my refuge. You alone are my safety. You—alone—are enough for me. Amen.

Chapter 19

Helping Parents Choose
Their Friends Wisely

Love . . . does not envy, it does not boast, it is not proud.
1 Corinthians 13:4

All of us are people of influence. All of us are
trying to make sense out of life and sharing our
interpretations with others. The giving and receiving
of counsel is the stuff of human relationships.
Paul David Tripp

If you've ever been around someone, worked with someone, been married to someone, or was born to someone
who never feels you're doing "enough" for them, then this
story is for you. My friend Mark is one standup guy. He is
married to a wonderful woman, Teresa, and together they
keep close tabs on Mark's elderly folks. Mark and Teresa
single-handedly care for Mark's parents, even though Mark
has siblings who could help. His parents still live in their
own home and have no plans to move into any type of
assisted-living facility. Instead, Mark and Teresa are their
assisted-living facilitators.

Though both of my friends are officially retired, they continue to work from their home, volunteer in the community, and are actively involved in service at their church. They are wholeheartedly servant-minded individuals. So when I last inquired about Mark's folks, what they shared made me sick at heart.

Apparently, Mark's folks have "friends" who have been throwing monkey wrenches into just about every conversation Mark and Teresa have with his parents. It always seems to start off innocently enough, but within ten minutes the conversation is laced with subtle jabs that Mark isn't doing nearly enough. Or that Teresa really ought to give up her job to come over every day to spend time with them, just in case. At first, Mark was puzzled; he couldn't figure out why all of a sudden his parents had an attitude of entitlement. He and Teresa discussed the situation at length, looking for possible clues as to why his parents were now generally upset, ungrateful, and often accusatory.

Finally, Teresa caught wind of the source of the trouble: new neighbors. Mark's folks had brand-new neighbors who were also senior citizens, and Mark had initially thought, "Wonderful! New friends for Mom and Dad." Mark was wrong. These new neighbors did come over most afternoons to visit or play cards, but mostly they came to brag about their kids and grandkids. Mark's parents had only Mark and Teresa who cared about them. Seemingly innocent conversations had fueled a fire in Mark's parents' hearts, so that now they continually competed with their neighbors.

Once he realized what was happening, Mark had a long conversation with his parents. He sat them down and confronted them with their unrealistic expectations and wildly "off" comments about Mark and Teresa not caring about them. Mark also challenged his parents to be more discerning about whom they chose as friends. He pointedly asked his parents if their neighbors brought "life" into their lives or just negativity. It wasn't easy for Mark to open up this topic with his folks, but Mark wisely realized that if he didn't he'd soon start resenting his parents and the whole sinful cycle would just continue to escalate. Happily, Mark's parents thought long and hard about what Mark said to them about their friends. Soon afterward, they minimized the time they spent with the neighbors who had started all the drama.

❦

Interestingly, most of us have probably had at least one person in our lives who fits the characteristic of Mark's folks. No matter what you do, how often you visit, how many times you call, and how hard you work to make them comfortable, these not-to-be-pleased people are not-to-be pleased. The truth is that it's not your problem. It's theirs. Your mission is to define the role God has given you in relation to your parents at this time of their lives. Remember that the friends your folks surround themselves with will likely become a larger-than-life influence in theirs as they age.

Two primary repercussions develop when our elderly parents have friends who love to brag about their families (true or not): they raise our parents' expectations of us even when the scenarios are completely different. In Mark's case, it was only he and Teresa caring for his parents, whereas the new neighbors had a large family with around twenty grandchildren—and someone was always stopping over. This unfair comparison made anything Mark and Teresa did look poor in contrast.

Another potential pitfall of friends who don't think before they speak is that your aged parents' friends may start giving them advice on everything, from their housing to food choices, prescriptions, doctor's care, and so on. What to their elderly minds appear to be great solutions to troubling issues may not work out in real life.

Mark and Teresa were well aware of his parents' mental and physical health. They knew how much money they had and what type of health insurance coverage they relied on. All these important facts seemed to fly out the window when the neighbors began discussing and suggesting expensive and unrealistic options to Mark's folks. Mark and Teresa had to sit down and show them in black and white why they weren't eligible to try "this" or experiment with "that."

The bottom line is that choosing the right friends is important at every age. The people we spend the most time with influence us far more than we often realize. In truth, we become our friends. Mark realized that truth, and he rightfully stepped into an awkward conversation because he loved his parents enough to tell them the truth.

Take-away Action Thought

When I see new people enter my parents' lives, I will take the time to get to know them for myself before they gain admittance to the hearts of my loved ones. If need be, I will have a conversation with my parents if I start to see something negative happening.

My Heart's Cry to You, O Lord

You know I want my parents to have friends with whom they can enjoy life. But lately, I notice that some of these friends are bringing resentment into our relationship. My folks suddenly expect of us what we cannot give. Help me to be bold enough to speak the truth to my parents and confront them when they speak untruths. I love them deeply, but I cannot allow their friends to have more sway over their care than I do. Help me to trust you through this situation. Give me your wisdom to solve this problem in your way. Amen.

Chapter 20

When Parents Misunderstand or Become Confused

My flesh and my heart may fail,
   but God is the strength of my heart
   and my portion forever.
Psalm 73:26

*Every passing year increases my longing to live on
the resurrected Earth in my resurrected body with my
resurrected family and friends, worshiping and serving the
resurrected Jesus. I get goose bumps just thinking about it.*
Randy Alcorn

When I sat visiting with my friend Don, he told me about the time he had felt like he was on a virtual roller-coaster ride. His father had taken his mother to the doctor and when they came home, he frantically called all their friends and family, telling them she had been given a fatal diagnosis. Don got the call and raced over to his parents' house. When he arrived, his mother was sobbing and his father was pacing. Attempting to calm them down, he asked his father to tell him everything—to begin at the beginning.

Throughout her adult life, Don's mother had a history of kidney stones. Of late, she had been experiencing increasing back pain, so they made an appointment to see her urologist. The doctor did a KUB to see if she was passing another stone. She wasn't. It was something else, likely a benign cyst, but it needed further testing and a possible biopsy. That's what Don discovered after he called the urologist's office and found out the facts.

What Don's father told him was this: "Your mother has a cancerous tumor in her kidney, and they can't remove it so she is going to die." Quite a different interpretation of the true diagnosis. Don felt immediate relief after he had followed up with the doctor. But the next emotion Don felt wasn't relief—it was a sudden surge of adrenaline he recognized as an early warning alert system calling Don to take action.

Don understood that his father's mind had been failing some, but it was nothing to worry about yet. Still, after this blatant mistake of failing to hear correctly what their doctor was saying, and also misunderstanding the implications of his words, Don knew he had to start accompanying his parents to all their important appointments. Don thought about this emotional scenario long after his folks had forgotten it. He soberly realized that this is how elderly people get scammed when phone solicitors call and make threats or offer them unbelievable deals. Thankfully, Don's folks' situation didn't put into motion a series of unfortunate events—but it easily could have.

Aging alone can bring about significant lapses in the ability to hear, process, and decode information. Add in an illness or two, and a person's mental acuity becomes greatly diminished. Like Don experienced, there will come a day when elderly parents need help processing the information they read and hear. It may be a doctor's advice on taking medications, or the phone company offering a myriad of choices too confusing to understand, or even simple banking tasks that become a muddled mix of nonsensical numbers. Whatever the area of struggle, adult children need to keep a sharp eye on all the vital communication and information their parents need to process.

In Don's case, it was a relatively simple fix. All Don needed to do was call the doctor to obtain the facts. However, if Don hadn't earlier made sure his parents added his name to all their medical doctor's lists, he could have been left wondering how much of what his father said was true until they were able to see the doctor at another time.

It's much easier for everyone involved if at least one adult child is listed on all important legal papers, trusts, and checking/savings accounts, with the ability to obtain legal access so they can make decisions for their parents as warranted.

Take-away Action Thought

Today, I will make sure that someone in the family has the legal ability to help our parents make the needed decisions once they are unable to do so themselves. I also want to keep discussing their needs with my siblings so that we are all in agreement on our parents' care.

My Heart's Cry to You, O Lord

Thank you, Lord, for reminding me about the changes that are happening inside of my parents' minds. I suppose I've been receiving hints for a while that neither of them is as sharp as they used to be, though nothing major warranted my concern until now. Give me the wisdom to know how to best approach them with new information that may be hard for them to process. Help me to be patient when explaining different options and choices with them. And let me make prudent preparations for the day when they are unable to decide for themselves any longer. I rely on your wisdom, your strength, and your grace to handle all these changes without becoming overwhelmed myself. Amen.

Chapter 21

Grieving Together What Will Never Be Again

Though he brings grief, he will show compassion,
so great is his unfailing love.

Lamentations 3:32

Some people assume worry is the result of too
much thinking. Actually, it's the result of too little
thinking in the right direction. If you know who
God is and understand His purposes, promises,
and plans, it will help you not to worry.

John MacArthur

Jenny got up from her hands and knees and brushed off the dirt that clung to her. With a few brisk swipes, her hands were clean again. Too bad a few swift shakes couldn't heal how broken her heart felt these days. Looking over her bounteous garden, Jenny reflected how quickly the years had passed. How could it be that she was almost sixty? Jenny may not have looked her age on the outside, but anyone close to her recognized she was carrying a weighty burden on the inside these days.

Pushing herself to get on to the next outdoor task, Jenny began winding up the garden hoses and wheeling them to the backside of her pole barn. Out of sight, out of mind, she chuckled. Once again, Jenny's thoughts unconsciously pivoted right back to where they started—to thoughts of her good friend and older cousin, Ruth. It had been Ruth who had taken Jenny in when her mother and father split those many years ago. They divorced back in the days way before "getting a divorce" was almost as common as getting married. For several years, Jenny had been shuffled from one relative's home to the next. It wasn't until Ruth called a family meeting and said in her no-nonsense way, "Enough is enough—Jenny is moving home with me for good," that Jenny's life became something akin to normal.

Jenny had lived with Ruth until she graduated from college. Then the following year, Jenny married and began raising her own family only twenty miles from Ruth's home. Though Jenny and Ruth had stayed close, Jenny realized Ruth's failing health meant some major life changes. Jenny knew she was the one who needed to have "that conversation" with Cousin Ruth because they were closer than anyone else in the family. So why did she feel like she was betraying the woman who raised her like her own?

Knowing she couldn't put off the visit any longer, Jenny went inside the house, changed her clothes, gathered some extra meals she'd made for Ruth—and then tried to gather her courage. Knocking on Ruth's door, Jenny waited, and waited, and waited. Panic stricken, Jenny knocked harder. Receiving no answer, she ran around to the back of the house and looked for the spare key hidden under a garden ornament. Bending over with trembling fingers, Jenny snatched the key and raced back to the front door. She inserted the key and almost jumped back in fright when the door opened.

"Jenny!" exclaimed Ruth, "What are you doing here? You're supposed to be coming tomorrow."

Jenny caught her breath and shook her head. "No, Ruth, I told you I was coming over Tuesday morning after chores. Today is Tuesday—"

"But . . ." Ruth's voice lingered in confusion, "I thought it was . . ."

Jenny took Ruth by the hand, and together they looked at the calendar.

Ruth shook her head again. "I don't know how I got that mixed up . . ."

Jenny brought in the meals, put them away, and wrote down the reheating instructions for Ruth. They then sat outside and enjoyed a terrific conversation about all things garden related. After about an hour, Jenny felt much better about Ruth's state of mind. She was just a worrier. Ruth was fine—her forgetting this visit was merely a simple mistake.

Jenny put on her coat, picked up her purse, and said her goodbyes to Ruth. But as she walked away from the house, Ruth stood at the doorstep looking out at Jenny, greeting her as if she had just arrived. Jenny tried explaining to Ruth that they had already visited and that she was leaving, not arriving. Ruth look puzzled. Jenny even took Ruth into the kitchen and showed her the meals she had put away in the refrigerator. Ruth still looked blank. It was as though the last ninety minutes had never happened.

Startled and a bit frightened, Jenny didn't know what to do. She didn't want to leave Ruth alone. But Jenny had several appointments she needed to get to and a whole list of to-dos. And yet, there was no way she could leave Ruth unattended until they got to the bottom of her memory loss. Sending up a quick prayer, Jenny turned to Ruth and said, "Get your coat and purse. You're coming home with me today." Afraid Ruth would balk, Jenny waited for her reaction—but it turned out she didn't need to be anxious. Ruth just smiled and said, "Oh, Honey, I'll go anywhere with you."

Though Jenny did not yet realize it, she had just started on a long and heartbreaking journey with her beloved Ruth. Her older cousin's memory was simply beginning to fade away, and within a year, Ruth no longer knew who Jenny was. Before Ruth's ability to process thoughts and memories left her, however, she and Jenny spent many long hours talking about the past, laughing about current events, and speculating about the future. Though Ruth had wisely prepared for long-term care for herself, it was Jenny who struggled against the inevitable. Ruth told Jenny in her more cognizant moments, "There will come a day when I won't recognize you, and when that day arrives I probably won't listen to you either." Jenny knew what Ruth was saying. When Ruth's mind left her, it wouldn't be safe for her to be in Jenny's home—not with Jenny and the family in and out much of the time.

Jenny cried on the day they took Ruth to live in a nursing home with 24/7 care, but Ruth didn't cry. Her personality was so altered, she didn't seem aware of leaving Jenny or of moving into her new home. Jenny recalled later that one of the very best decisions she and Ruth made early on was to talk and remember and reflect. They had walked through their entire lives together. Together, both women grieved the loss they knew was coming. Together, they held hands and let the tears flow.

Once when Jenny was feeling especially anxious about what was coming, Ruth took her aside and again took on the mothering role, assuring Jenny: "I am not afraid. God is faithful and he'll never leave me, even if I am not aware of his presence." Jenny often reflected upon that final "mother moment" when Ruth gave her good counsel, wise thoughts, and the hope of a promised future in heaven where Ruth would be sound in both mind and body once again. Whenever Jenny feels low, she does what Ruth taught her to do: go out and spend some time digging in God's green earth, and then go out and find somebody who's hurting more than you are.

Take-away Action Thought

When I feel overwhelmed and discouraged,
I will redirect my thoughts to the unfailing
faithfulness of God, past and present and future.
I need to remember that we age and that this
doesn't change the fact that he will always be
with us, even if we can no longer think clearly.

My Heart's Cry to You, O Lord

Today, you know that I'm feeling sad and anxious and maybe even a little guilty. Lord, even though I can sit quietly and remember many wonderful moments with my loved one, it's not the same as being able to have those same experiences today. Help me to grow a deeply thankful heart for every single second I lived loved by my family and friends. Give me the wisdom to take time to sit and really converse with anyone and everyone you've placed in my path today. Finally, Lord, help me to not worry about how fast life and relationships can change from day to day. Rather, give me your peace of mind in abundance and help me rest securely there. Amen.

Chapter 22

Gently Challenging Parents to Keep Using Their Gifts and Talents

Each of you should use whatever gift you
have received to serve others.
1 Peter 4:10

*The most radical treatment for the fear of man
is the fear of the Lord. God must be bigger to
you than people are. This antidote takes years
to grasp; in fact, it will take all of our lives.*
Edward Welch

You never know what is going to come out of people's
mouths. The last thing I ever expected Seth to say was that
he was so angry with his mother he could spit. I almost
expected him to do so right then and there.

Here's the backstory. Seth's mother had been an active
member in her church, volunteering for any and all "help
wanted" positions for over fifty years. Most definitely, she
had the gift of "helps" and lived for expressing this ben-
eficial attribute toward anyone with whom she came into
contact. Until five years ago, when her husband died.

After her husband's passing, Seth's mother sort of died too. Her health was robust, her mind intact, her skills and natural abilities never waned—but her heart just wasn't in anything anymore. Seth felt he could almost have lived with his mother's changes except that every time he read the 1 Peter passage cited above, his thoughts turned to his mother. He hated the fact that with all her former "experience" in meeting a variety of needs inside the church walls and outside it, she now did nothing. And seemingly nothing would persuade her to leave her house.

Seth was so frustrated with her inactivity and lack of service that he became majorly distracted by it. It was a problem that needed to be fixed sooner than later. Seth tried everything he could think of to re-involve his mother in her former happy service activities. But her only response to him was: "I can't do that," or "I'm not comfortable trying that."

After many trial and error conversations, Seth finely got to the bottom of it all: his mother was afraid she was losing her "touch," or her skills and abilities. She was feeling her age and fearful of getting into something where she might fail. That Seth could understand, and he explained to her that everyone feels that way. We're all fearful of making mistakes and looking foolish. However, we mustn't let that stop us from obeying God's commands. He has gifted each of us with skills and abilities so we might use them to serve others, to meet others' needs. After Seth challenged his mother with this truth, he swears he saw a brief twinkle in her eyes. Maybe, just maybe, she'll listen to me this time, Seth hopes. But if not, he's ready to bring their pastor along for the next conversation.

The twists and turns of aging take so many different circuitous routes. I'm amazed how once talented, involved people suddenly decide to stay home and do nothing. Naturally, if illness (mental or physical) occurs, then these drastic changes make sense. But a sudden about-face from being regularly involved to hibernating at home signals something wrong. I so appreciated Seth's tenacious spirit in challenging his mother to keep serving since she is able-bodied. I love the fact that he was able to remind his mother of Scripture's commands to go and serve. And that once he did this, he did in fact begin to see her taking note of his words of admonition to her.

Whether we like it or not, aging ushers in all sorts of new challenges. Some are real—and others are only real in our minds. Seth's mother had (and has) so much to give. Sadly, she gave way to fear: fear of failure, fear of rejection, fear of people. Over and over in Scripture, we are reminded that fear of people will be anyone's downfall. God must be big. People must be small. When we view God as big, even our failures pale in light of our obedience to him.

As Seth experienced, learning to fear God alone will take our entire lives to master. Even as aged as Seth's mother was, she struggled with the possibility of making a mistake and appearing foolish. This makes me wonder how many other senior citizens truly want to get involved in their church and community but allow fear to stop them. We all need a Seth in our lives to keep us sharp and accountable for God's glory and our good.

Take-away Action Thought

When I become frustrated with my parents'
lack of service to others, I will first of all pray
before I speak to them about it. Next, I will
ask specific questions to try to get to the real
reason why they have ceased the activities that
always brought them so much satisfaction.

My Heart's Cry to You, O Lord

Today, I struggled yet again with patience. I'm sorry
for the rising irritability I feel most of the time when I'm
with my folks. I just don't understand how people who are
healthy and strong can willingly opt out of life and church
and being helpful to others. Your word, Lord, is so clear
about using our gifts to be of service to those around us.
How can my parents, who raised me to live this way, be
so blind to their own disobedience? No one ever "retires"
from serving God and others. Help me, Lord, to find the
right words and the best way to tackle this touchy subject,
when the time is right. Amen.

Chapter 23

Expecting the Unexpected

Love is patient, love is kind.
1 Corinthians 13:4

*Taking up our crosses daily doesn't mean making one
big once-and-for-all sacrifice and getting it over with.
It means repeatedly, over and over again, day after
day and year after year, saying no to present desires
and plans in order to say yes to God and others.*
Randy Alcorn

Earlier in the summer, my friend Brad had this grand idea of helping his eighty-two-year-old father celebrate his birthday in a big way. Brad's father has been a widower for over fifteen years; and as the years went by, it became obvious that this once life-of-the-party man had become a loner. Although Brad and his siblings have tried their level best to get their father out and about on a regular basis, he has wanted nothing to do with their ideas.

Brad has finally made some progress, though, and is thankful that his father is back to attending church with them on a regular basis. He has even willingly come to all the recent family birthday parties and other holiday celebrations. After one such event, Brad's father remarked that he was sorry he had missed out on attending these gatherings in the past. He realized after a friend passed away suddenly that he wanted to relish each day with Brad and his other children.

Brad felt his emotions soar after this conversation and decided then and there that he would make certain to celebrate his father's upcoming birthday in style. Brad and his wife sent out formal invitations to family and friends. He rented a small hall, catered the food, and everyone promised to bring a birthday card complete with a special memory written inside. Brad even ordered a huge birthday cake in his father's favorite flavor. As the days preceding his father's birthday approached, Brad's excitement increased.

On the morning of the party, Brad told his father he would pick him up to bring him over to Brad's house for dinner. Brad arrived at his father's home and found his father still in his pajamas. He tried to get his father dressed, but he refused—adamantly: "I just don't feel like going . . ."

It didn't matter what Brad said to try and convince his father to get up and get ready; he wasn't about to budge. Brad felt his anger rise as he considered the group of people all eagerly awaiting their arrival. He also felt frustrated, irritated, and a genuine lack of compassion for his father in that moment. After a good forty-five minutes of attempting to cajole his father into coming, Brad finally told his father about the surprise party. Instead of changing his mind, this made his father dig his heels in further. "I told you, I'm not going!" His father stated this so strongly that Brad knew the discussion was over.

Driving to the rented hall, Brad tried to come up with a good reason to explain away why he didn't have his father with him. But he just couldn't come up with one.

※

As Brad experienced, honing an attitude of flexibility might be the saving grace in a relationship with an aging parent whose personality and likes/dislikes change with each passing day. Brad only wants what is best for his father, but he discovered after investing significant time and money (not to mention his emotional investment) that plans don't always turn out as we hoped.

Perhaps the better way to tackle these ever-altering daily preferences is to expect the unexpected and not be surprised when a 180 degree turn happens. We can know someone intimately and learn to anticipate what they like/dislike. Yet as older age takes hold, not only might preferences change, but whole personalities can disappear while others take their place.

Brad realized another truth. He needed to hone a robust sense of humor too. Instead of wasting too much time and energy trying to convince his father of something, Brad learned to shrug off possible areas of contention before they turned into full-blown arguments that frustrated both of them. Brad wisely understood that his father may not be able to explain why he doesn't want to participate in certain activities anymore, but Brad had to accept it and honor his father's choices.

For the record, Brad handled the whole situation like a champ. His friends and family were surprised at first when he arrived alone at the party. But after the first few stunned moments of silence, laughter erupted in its place and the group had a memorable afternoon. After all, who is going forget attending a birthday party that the guest of honor refused to attend?

Take-away Action Thought

When I'm left confused by the preferences of my parents, I will not push them into something they don't want to do. Instead, I will graciously leave the choice up to them.

My Heart's Cry to You, O Lord

Father, help me to have an attitude of flexibility when it comes to the changing likes and dislikes that my parents voice to me. I may not fully understand why they feel as they do, but I can choose to let it go and not make an issue of it. Help me to use wisdom and compassion as my guide when I offer suggestions or options to them. I don't want to get frustrated when they suddenly alter their habits or patterns. Give me a servant's heart in all situations, knowing full well that you govern our lives well. Amen.

Chapter 24

Helping Them Make Difficult Decisions

LORD, be gracious to us;
    we long for you.
Be our strength every morning,
    our salvation in time of distress.

Isaiah 33:2

The one to whom we pray knows our feelings.
He knows temptation. He has felt discouraged. He
has been hungry and sleepy and tired. . . . He nods
in understanding when we pray in anger . . . he
smiles when we confess our weariness.

Max Lucado

Ana was overwhelmed by the offers coming her way—she couldn't and honestly didn't know how to process all this information. Everything sounded too good to be true. How could she ever make a decision? Ana had until the weekend to decide whether or not her mother would take the opening at a local nursing home facility. Her mother had placed herself on the waiting list some years earlier. Not wanting to burden any of her grown children with her end-of-life care, she was ever so thoughtful. But suddenly, when it came down to actually signing the papers, her mother admitted to some hesitancy. Thus Ana's last minute scramble to find alternatives.

Ana, her siblings, and her mother all agreed that it wasn't safe for her to live alone any longer. So, when this well-coveted spot opened up, everyone felt relieved. That's when Ana's mother began to have second thoughts, and understandably so. With three of the four adult children living out of state, it was left to Ana to do all the legwork. She had spent the last couple of days on the phone calling every agency she could find to get their quotes on in-home health care. With Ana working part-time days, her mother truly needed another adult in her home from 9:00 to 5:00. In the evenings, Ana and her kids could take turns getting her mother into bed at 8:00 p.m. She also had an emergency monitor near her bed in case she needed help during the night.

The hardest part of making this decision was that her mother was mourning the potential loss of her home and her independence in one fell swoop. Ana's mother had the money for in-home health care during the day, as it was something she had set aside and planned for over the years. Still, Ana balked at paying out so much money every week. It seemed like such a waste, especially since she and her kids would be over so much in the evenings. Exasperated, Ana pushed herself away from the pile of lists in front of her and closed her eyes. The only solution she could think of was for her to move into Mom's house, at least temporarily. She could not, however, make this major decision over the span of one weekend—it was too much for her and even more stress on her mother.

※

During times of sudden crisis, it is natural to call in the experts. Everyone feels more comfortable getting information from folks who specialize in the problem we're trying to solve. In fact, many people defer to the experts' opinions, even against their own better judgment. Ana was facing a major life choice that would affect her mother for the rest of her life. Even though her mother had previously planned on retiring to a certain nursing home in her last days, when the opportunity arose, she found herself changing her mind. Ana, trying to make the best decision based on all the facts, ended up making the best decision based on knowing her mother best.

In other words, it's a good call to call in experts in times of trouble. It is important to weigh all the options we have before coming to a decision. However, all the experts in the world do not know your parents as you do. Ana took the information she had gathered and weighed it against the intimate knowledge she had of her mother. Ana knew that moving her into a nursing care facility before she was ready might literally kill her—that is, at least her will to live. Ana wisely took a stand based on facts mixed with love and chose a different option. She realized it wasn't a permanent fix, but for the time being Ana would make it work. Ana, for one, never liked being forced into a life-altering choice on such short notice.

Take-away Action Thought

When too much information comes my way, I will purposefully stop, pray, and wait on God to guide me. I will compile all the information together and then let it sit for a time, while I continue to think and pray for the best outcome.

My Heart's Cry to You, O Lord

Father, in the last few days, so much information has been thrust at me that I'm feeling overwhelmed and confused by it all. Help me to unravel all these numbers and options and simplify the choices before me. Remind me to keep in mind my parent's desires and wishes too. In some way, I know you will guide me and my thoughts so that I am able to do the best for my parent given my options. Help me to think outside the box and find creative ways to meet her needs. I rely on you, Lord, always—and especially now, when the future of my loved one and her happiness is at stake. Amen.

Chapter 25

Grieving the Loss of a Loved One

Your word is a lamp for my feet
and a light on my path.
Psalm 119:105

When you hurt, God hurts with you.
Max Lucado

Holly's parents were in their early eighties and, until last year, both had been in fine health. Sure, they had their aches and pains, but neither one had ever been hospitalized or undergone any surgeries. Holly fully expected her folks to live well into their nineties, and they might have if it hadn't been for the car accident. Her parents were on their way to the grocery store in broad daylight and perfect weather conditions. It wasn't their fault that a young mother with a couple of toddlers ran a stop sign and careened right into their vehicle.

While no one died in the crash, Holly's mother broke her hip and never fully recovered after her surgery. Holly visited her mother almost daily in rehab and would swing by to pick up her father on the way. For a while it looked like her mother would make a full recovery. Then one after another, minor mishaps kept occurring. First, she contracted a virus that left her weak. Next, it was a bacterial infection, and finally a blood clot was discovered. Holly grew weary and disheartened by this constant stream of setbacks, as did her father.

Holly later admitted there were moments when she simply prayed that the Lord would call her mother home. Then Holly would feel guilty for thinking such a thought and praying such a prayer. She knew her father was lonely and depressed being by himself all day long. Holly tried to cheer him up and include him in her family's activities, but all he wanted to do was sit by his wife—which was completely understandable.

Then one late winter evening, Holly got the call that her mother had passed away. After she had hung up the phone and cried, shedding all the tears still left in her after this long ordeal, she drove over to her father's and broke the news to him. Of course, her father wept alongside Holly's fresh torrent of tears. Holly didn't know if she had ever felt such pity for another person in her entire life. Sitting there trying to console him tore her own heart into pieces.

Holly spent the remainder of the night with her father. The next morning there were funeral details to attend to, family to call, plans to make. Together, Holly and her father soldiered through the following days in a daze. After the funeral, Holly realized some of the most difficult days were yet to come.

Life is always throwing the unexpected our way. Thankfully, Holly was as prepared as anyone could be to face one of the hardest events in life: death. Her faith was robust, and she knew her parents were ready to face eternity because they knew Jesus as their Savior. But still, can anyone really be ready to say goodbye to a loved one?

As Holly discovered, as much pain as she was experiencing, her father felt it even more keenly because of the marital bond. They had spent their entire adult lives together, sharing the ups and downs of daily life as a couple. Holly felt sorrow, and then she felt burdensome pain for her father. In the coming weeks and months, Holly knew much of her available time and energy would be going toward helping him adjust to life as a widower. Often, she knew they would need to sit down, open up the Bible, and read aloud God's promises to sustain them during their sorrow and to remind them of the upcoming joys of eternity. Holly was confident of one thing: God would be faithful to show himself strong on her father's behalf until the day he called her father into eternity too.

Take-away Action Thought

When I face the most difficult moments in life,
I will turn my face toward the Light. I need
to find my solace and strength in God and in
his word, and then pass it on to my family.

My Heart's Cry to You, O Lord

Today I had to face the passing of one of my parents, and the hardest part was telling my other parent the news. Father, I so needed your strength today. When I heard the news, I wanted to retreat into a quiet place by myself and mourn my loss in private. But that wasn't an option. In the days to come, help me to stay sensitive to the needs of my remaining parent. Help me to take all the time needed to listen, to pray, and to simply be there. Let me not forget that while I have lost a parent, he has lost a spouse, a life-long companion. Give me your words to provide comfort, to ease the pain, and to bring the hope of eternity home to my loved one. Amen.

Chapter 26

Sometimes We Get What We Least Expected

Love covers over all wrongs.
Proverbs 10:12

We come into the world needy, and we leave it the same way. Without suffering we would forget our neediness. If suffering seems too high a price for faith, it's because we underestimate faith's value.

Randy Alcorn

Twice a year, my good friend Maggie breezes into town for a weekend to visit with old friends before she drives south to spend time with her mother- and father-in-law. Maggie used to jokingly say she needed an emotional/spiritual fuel-up before tackling a week with her in-laws, specifically her mother-in-law. But no more.

Some ten or so years earlier, Maggie's cantankerous mother-in-law had a stroke that left her paralyzed on one side—and completely changed on the inside. Before the stroke, Maggie, as sweet a woman as you'd ever meet, had done her best to overcome her mother-in-law's unkind disposition. Maggie had intellectually understood that her husband's mother wasn't just mean to her—she was abrupt, demanding, judgmental, and pretty much unkind to everyone.

Still, it upset my dear friend to no end that no matter how hard she tried, her mother-in-law had remained aloof at best. I still remember holding Maggie's hand and hugging her before she ventured south on her twice-yearly jaunts home. We all promised to pray Maggie through her visits. Still, it was never easy, and Maggie rarely ended a visit without tears stinging her cheeks.

In her heart of hearts, Maggie had always hoped she would enjoy an intimate relationship with the mother of the man she married. Maggie's own mother had passed away before she even walked down the aisle. So from the get-go, her mother-in-law was the only female in the immediate family circle. Maggie's husband and her father-in-law often made apologies for her behavior, which had helped a little.

But with the stroke, all this had changed. In God's grand scheme of life, something seemingly catastrophic had transpired to dramatically change Maggie's mother-in-law's personality for the better. No longer does Maggie dread these visits home. Instead, she has become strangely excited and looks forward to this new relationship she is enjoying with her mother-in-law. Maggie often wonders out loud if there is some science behind her mother-in-law's change in personality due to her stroke. But honestly, it doesn't really matter, does it?

Maggie now feels almost like a kid in a candy store when she visits. Her mother-in-law greets her with warm hugs and sloppy kisses. She thoughtfully stocks their kitchen with Maggie's favorites, and Maggie has even discovered special small gifts scattered around the bedroom they use when visiting.

Though Maggie would never have wanted to endure all those hard years with her mother-in-law, she secretly feels like God is making up for all those years of rejection, harshness, and coldness. Only God. Maggie has said that many times during our short catch-up conversations of late. And she's right. Only God.

Expectations are tricky. We are correct in having healthy expectations in our relationships. We teach our sons and daughters to treat others with dignity and respect. We offer them real-life examples of what this looks like in the personal and working world. We instruct them in proper ways of handling those uncomfortable (and hurtful) situations where respect is not given. In every way possible, we attempt to prepare our children to face those who won't treat them well.

So what happens when an older parent or relative begins exhibiting the poor behavior we've lectured our kids about? How do we handle it? Whatever game plan we come up with, on an emotional level it's never easy to execute. Like Maggie, we all hope to have healthy and mutually edifying relationships with aging parents and in-laws. Also, like Maggie, some of us will be treated in the same unkind manner she had to endure until her mother-in-law's stroke.

There is no simple fix to those difficult relationships with even more difficult people. I'm always reminded of the passage in Scripture where it talks about living peaceably with all people as much as it is possible. Which assumes the obvious: some folks don't live in peace with anyone. I've discovered along the way that when I'm dealing with prickly people, it's best if I go into the relationship with my eyes wide open. It's not that I'm expecting "evil" of someone; rather, I'm prepared to hold the line when needed. I'm ready to set up healthy boundaries. I'm ready for "battle" if necessary by praying before I "engage" with the "enemy."

While we all long for quality family relationships, the hard reality is that many of us may never experience them. Sure, we may relish today's peaceful moment, but an illness may suddenly rob us of our loved one's good temperament permanently.

Maggie was blessed by her mother-in-law's reversal of personality, but it's usually the other way round. For those other times, how do we continue to love our loved one when they stop loving us? By following Maggie's fine example of pursuing peace with gracious intentionally, we can find practical ways to demonstrate that we care. By committing ourselves to hang in there for the long haul no matter what, we can overcome evil with good.

Certainly, we pray and hope for the best. But even if the worst comes to pass, God can and will supply us with what we need to get the job done. He always has done so. He always will do so. Disappointments and personal pain aside, God equips us completely when he calls us into his service.

Take-away Action Thought

When I feel disappointed in a relationship,
I will take my expectations to God and
believe that while there is still breath in
a body, change is always possible.

My Heart's Cry to You, O Lord

Help me to not become weary in doing good to those you have placed in my life. Lord, I need your unconditional love, constant strength, and mercy to keep on serving when I receive nothing but rejection in response. Show me how to love the unlovable. Give me everything I need to press past my personal hurts to see how deeply injured this other person truly is on the inside. Let me remember your example of laying down your life for us, Lord. Oh, I recognize how much I need you—every hour I need you. Amen.

Chapter 27

Remembering that Each Generation Is Different

I will deliver this people from the power
   of the grave;
  I will redeem them from death.
Where O death, are your plagues?
   Where, O grave, is your destruction?

Hosea 13:14

*There are moments in life when God's goodness and love
seem to come under a blackout. No matter how we strain
our eyes, we cannot see any good, not a trace of God's love.
Faith, in the final analysis, is trusting someone you know,
even when you don't always understand what he is doing.*

Carolyn Custis James

I felt like laughing, but I didn't. It was a standing joke between me and my good friend, Renee. Every Thursday, come rain or shine, Renee's mother would leave her a voice message confirming their standing Saturday morning breakfast date—their visit to the cemetery. Like many younger folks, Renee still doesn't fully understand the draw to visit her father's grave week in and week out. Sure, she'll place seasonal bouquets of flowers in the vase near his headstone marking where he was buried some fifteen years ago. But every week?

Renee and I have discussed this habitual cemetery visitation many times. We've noticed that very few of our contemporaries find it necessary or comforting to repeatedly visit the gravesite of deceased family members. As far as we can tell, those of us in the Baby Boomer age range aren't cemetery regulars. What we have also noticed is that the generation before ours does in fact make cemetery visiting a regular priority. We admittedly find it strange.

Renee confides in me that it takes all of her (limited) patience (her words, not mine) to drive through those wrought-iron gates every Saturday morning. Since her mother cannot drive, Renee feels obligated to take her. I asked Renee if she'd ever tackled the topic with her mother to better understand why these weekly visits matter. After all, Renee's mother is a Christian, as was her father, so she knows he isn't there waiting for her to arrive with family updates.

After a few such probing conversations, Renee admitted she didn't get a whole lot of insight into this ritual other than: "It makes me feel closer to your father." Renee also picked up on the fact that each time they ventured closer to her father's grave, her mother would begin reminiscing and retelling stories of memories from years gone by. Renee shared with me that it was on these early morning trips that her mother seemed to share more family history than at any other time.

Bingo! After Renee spoke those words, we both understood. That had to be it: visiting her father's gravesite sparked a multitude of memories for her mother. We discussed it further and agreed that the combination of a shared meal, a shared visit, and shared conversation did in fact spark her mother's memory in vivid ways. Renee began to see the value (to her mother and to herself) of these weekly treks to the cemetery. Not only did Renee learn lots of fascinating tidbits of family history on these Saturday mornings, she soon realized she and her mother were creating new memories between themselves. Memories, Renee understood, that she would one day soon cherish on her own terms.

It's true of every generation. No matter what era we were brought up in, each of us has certain specific and unique generational differences that we cherish—albeit there are some quirky ways we choose to express ourselves, our beliefs, and our patterns of living. However, these traditions in part reflect when we were born, where we grew up, and how we were taught.

Like Renee, I've witnessed the same desire to make consistent and frequent visits to a family gravesite. It's not that I totally understand it, but I respect it. I (and possibly many of my contemporaries) choose to remember deceased loves ones differently. The times I've spent accompanying older relatives at gravesites do nothing to comfort me. In fact, these experiences tend to leave me feeling blank. I'd much rather go through old photos, recalling specific moments in time when we were together, dusting the various pieces of furniture my family gave me, or recreating their favorite recipes in the kitchen to share with my spouse and children.

The point is every generation holds their own traditions dear to them. While I may not get the warm fuzzies at a gravesite, I surely can respect those who do and honor their choices. As I age, who knows how my own acts of remembrance might change? Finally, it may come full circle when my children and grandchildren are grown up. They may surprise me by reinstating the weekly visits to the family gravesite.

Take-away Action Thought

Even when I may not fully understand the "why" behind specific traditions, I will respect and honor them for the sake of my loved ones.

My Heart's Cry to You, O Lord

Father, I sometimes shake my head in confusion and, honestly, in impatience when my loved ones want to repeat the same tradition over and over again. It seems meaningless to me. I realize, however, that I need to honor and respect their wishes and comply as much as I am able. This is so hard for me to do. Please supply me with all the compassion and grace I require to keep on giving, even when I don't feel the value or importance of what has been requested of me. Thank you, Lord, in advance for all the strength and eternal perspective I am confident you will give me as each need arises. Amen.

Chapter 28

Sharing Your Faith with Unbelieving Parents

Lord, let your ear be attentive to the prayer of this your
servant and to the prayer of your servants who delight
in revering your name. Give your servant success today
by granting him favor in the presence of this man.

Nehemiah 1:11

*O God, do whatever is necessary to bring him to
repentance and faith in Your Son! It is in the powerful
name of the Lord Jesus Christ that I pray. Amen.*

Richard Burr

It was one of the fervent prayers of my heart that my
best friend's father would come to know Christ before he
died. My friend and I had been close since I was only five
years old and she was only seven. Since we'd been through
the highs and lows of life for over fifty years together, this
was one prayer heavy on both of our hearts. I couldn't tell
you exactly when we started praying for her father, but it
was many years ago.

My friend was the only one of her siblings who lived in
the area, so it was her responsibility to care for and watch

over her parents. Once her father's health diminished to the point where her mother couldn't care for him, he was placed in a nursing home. My friend visited him several times a week and sat talking about her family's current happenings. Sometimes he was coherent; other times not so much. Still, the burden of eternity weighed heavy on my friend's heart.

She had tried talking to her father about Christ to no avail. She had brought him books to read in earlier days, which he had dismissed offhandedly. Now, at his weakest point in his life, she wondered if someone else might possibly succeed where she had failed. She called a friend and pastor to visit her father one evening. He shared the gospel with her father and during that conversation, he accepted Christ as his Savior. "I've been waiting to hear this my whole life," he said.

Rejoicing over this news, we afterward often discussed how God truly does use one person to plant a seed, another to water, and another to reap the harvest. It is amazing. Her father's story continually gives me great reason for hope because there are so many in my life who haven't made the eternal decision to follow Christ. On days when I'm weary of praying, I call to mind my friend's father who literally on his deathbed cried out for salvation.

※

There is one lesson I have learned above all others: Never stop interceding for the lives of people without Christ. No matter how long you've prayed. No matter if you haven't seen any evidence of an answer to your prayers. Never,

ever give up. Someone, possibly many someones, prayed for you before you made a decision to follow Christ. Others faithfully invested themselves on your behalf. Never, ever give up.

I also discovered that I should never underestimate the small kindnesses we can offer to others in our path. We never know what part God has deemed we will play in someone else's life and their decision to accept Christ as their Savior. We may be the first to plant the seed. We may water the plant along the way. And possibly, we may be the one who will invite them to open their heart to Christ.

The old saying holds true for spiritual work too: "Many hands make light work." May our many prayers be continually lifted to the One who hears and answers. May our many acts of service and love break down the walls of suffering and pain. May our commitment to continue hoping never waver even in the face of adversity, discouragement, and distress. Let our best and final act be to keep lifting up the lost to the One who can find them, forgive them, and save them. Amen.

Take-away Action Thought

No matter how discouraged I am, I will never
stop praying for my lost loved ones. Each
and every day I will get up and pray for
those I love who haven't yet met Jesus.

My Heart's Cry to You, O Lord

Help me to be consistent in my pleas for the salvation of my loved ones. Give me a sense of your urgency, Lord, and your love for them. Help me to sacrifice other activities and take the time to intercede as your Holy Spirit moves me to do so. I want to storm the gates with my prayers and believe with all my heart that there is hope until the final breath is gone. I want to stand before you someday and witness how many people are there because you moved me to keep praying until you convinced them of your love. Remind me daily that the end of the story is never written until you say so. Amen.

Chapter 29

Guiding Parents through Their Limitations

You whom I have upheld since your birth,
  and have carried since you were born.
Even to your old age and gray hairs
  I am he, I am he who will sustain you.
I have made you and I will carry you;
  I will sustain you and I will rescue you.

Isaiah 46:3b–4

*Leave the broken, irreversible past in His hands, and
step out into the invincible future with Him.*

Oswald Chambers

You never know when you'll need to hone skills you learned from childhood on, because somebody important to you may depend upon it. Nicole was a successful food writer who helped prepare her local television's various anchors to create lavish holiday and party meal specials. Nicole worked from one major holiday to the next researching the best-tasting, most-nutritious (and cost-conscious) meals for their viewers. She loved her job, even though it meant long hours and little time for her to prepare her own meals.

Nicole recalls the day when she went to check in on her mother a few months after her father had passed away. Her mother looked peaked, thinner, and just not healthy. Nicole asked her mother if she was feeling well. Nicole's mother said she was feeling fine; she just didn't have as much get-up-and-go as usual. Nicole then took a closer look around her mother's apartment and noticed it was dusty, the carpet hadn't been swept, and the bathroom was getting a little grungy. So Nicole spent the next hour or so cleaning each room.

Next, Nicole looked into her mother's refrigerator and was shocked to find not much in there. "Mom, where's all your food? What have you eaten today?" When Nicole's mother shrugged indifferently, Nicole knew it was time for her to take a hand at making sure her mother's basic needs were getting met, because it was obvious her mother wasn't going to tell Nicole what she needed. Nicole sat down, and together they made out a grocery list that included easy items for healthy breakfasts and lunches. Then Nicole told her mother that she would start coming over once a week after work to cook with her. Nicole figured her own diet could use a healthy overhaul and now was the perfect time to start eating healthier and to get her mother to do the same.

From that week onward, Nicole was as good as her word. She would spend a little time on the weekend planning a few healthy meals that could stretch all week. She would shop for the ingredients on Monday. Then on Tuesday, she and her mother would spend a couple of hours prepping meals together and packaging them into individual-size portions. Whatever was left over, they'd freeze. Nicole was delighted to get back into the kitchen for herself (outside of work), and her mother was simply overjoyed that she and Nicole could look forward to that one evening a week when they were back in the kitchen cooking, baking, and simply relishing a home-cooked meal—together.

What I love most about this heartwarming story is Nicole's ingenuity. She took a problem, found a solution that benefited her and her mother, and then she executed it. While not every problem will be so simply solved, this is just one example of how a potentially problematic issue can be transformed into a blessing for everyone. Nicole chose a task she was good at (cooking and developing healthy meal plans on a budget) and ran with it. She also knew her mother needed help keeping the apartment clean. But instead of taking this task on for herself, she hired a college student she knew to come in once a week and do all the regular cleaning chores, as well as a load or two of laundry. Nicole's mother now had visitors at least twice a week, sometimes more.

Nicole's coworker, Alice, also took care of her parents and passed on a practical suggestion to her regarding meal prep. She reminded Nicole that older people generally have smaller appetites as they age. Instead of burdening them with a whole pan of lasagna or a large company-size casserole, Alice would divvy up these larger portions into single-size servings and freeze them. Alice shared with Nicole that she often spent an afternoon making four or more meals, kept half for her family, and packaged up the other half for her parents to unfreeze as needed. In this way, everybody wins.

Take-away Action Thought

If I'm unsure about whether or not
my parents are taking good care of
themselves, I'll do some detective work
of my own by closely inspecting them.

My Heart's Cry to You, O Lord

Father, help me to be keenly sensitive to the changing needs of my parents. I have to remind myself that the tasks they are able to handle this week may be too much for them next week. Help me to keep a lookout for anything that appears out of order, unkempt, or dirty. Show me things I may not spot on my own and give me sensitivity when discussing these issues with my folks. When new needs arise, I rely upon your creative wisdom and problem solving to guide me to the best solution. Keep reminding me to pray about everything, and let nothing cause me to fear. You have promised to care for each of us our entire lives. Thank you for this faithful word. Amen.

Chapter 30

When Parents Come between Their Children

A heart at peace gives life to the body,
but envy rots the bones.

Proverbs 14:30

*God will not simply wait for our deaths, then
snap his fingers to make us what he wants us to
be. He begins that process here and now, using
our suffering to help us grow in Christlikeness.*

Randy Alcorn

When Diane called me, I swear I felt the static run right through my phone and crackle as she spoke. It had happened again. My friend Diane, her family's relegated peacemaker, had suddenly become the scapegoat. A recently retired nurse, she was so looking forward to this new season of her life when she actually would have both time and energy (on the same day!) to pursue some long postponed dreams. Diane and her husband also wanted to travel to the different parts of the country where their three children had settled, married, and had their own children. Diane had worked at a local hospital for over thirty-five years, and she was ready to unleash a whole lot of creative energy in a variety of ways.

Unfortunately, at almost the same time Diane retired, her parents began having serious health problems. She had no problem helping out and even being the one to oversee their care—she was a nurse after all, and it was easy for her to assess a situation and then make the right health-care calls. The problem was Diane's brothers, who lived nearby but rarely took the time to visit or check in with their folks. It had been Diane who called them both and alerted them to their parents' recent medical issues. One brother promised to show up on the weekend to see "What's what." The other said he would try to fit in a call over the next week.

When Diane communicated her brothers' comments to her parents, they went into a rage. At first, Diane thought they were angry at her brothers' inactivity and lack of caring. Nope. They were fuming that *Diane* had somehow failed to communicate to her brothers how very ill they were and that *Diane* hadn't persuaded them to rush over. Stunned for a moment, she then started posing questions, reminding them that she couldn't force her brothers to do anything. After about an hour of useless, this-is-getting-us-nowhere conversation, Diane excused herself and left.

Two days later, Diane received not one but two irate voicemails from her brothers, who accused her of trying to stir up trouble between them and their parents. That was complete rubbish. Smack-dab in the middle of four unreasonable people who only thought of themselves, Diane decided to call a family meeting. She didn't hold out much hope that any of them would see her side of the situation, but she decided to try. She knew that if she didn't make the attempt to get everyone to see the problem accurately, then she would regret it. "At least," Diane told me, "I'll know I've given it my best shot, and we'll all know where we stand."

❧

Perhaps the most ludicrous aspect of Diane's problem was that her parents were the ones instigating a fight between their own adult children. Their accusations, while untrue, only served to stir up trouble between their would-be caregivers. But Diane is not alone in her situation. There are many families who operate in the same sinful manner. One adult child takes on the bulk of the caregiving, while the other children rarely make contact with their aged parents. But when they do deign to show up, the parents make a fuss over their presence.

This strangely unnatural attention awarded the "favored child" doesn't make any sense. Further, it frequently causes the faithful adult child emotional pain. They wonder why their aged parents only complain to them and about them. They start to think that if they stepped out of the picture for a while, then they might receive a warmer welcome when they did show up.

Another complication arises when the absent adult child appears and starts questioning (grilling) the caregiver child on everything he or she is doing. Again, this selfish and misguided approach causes only more strife within the family unit. There is so much about taking care of aging parents that defies common sense. As one good friend told me, "Stop trying to make sense of it. Just do your part and don't waste time or energy attempting to figure out why people do what they do at this stage in life." Easier said than done? Absolutely. As I encouraged Diane: "You can be at peace in your heart because you know you are doing everything you can for your parents. And that alone allows you to sleep at night."

Take-away Action Thought

When I find myself in the middle of a family mess not of my making, I will guard my heart and place my hope and confidence in God alone. I refuse to become embroiled in family feuds that benefit no one.

My Heart's Cry to You, O Lord

Lord, I used to long for peace to exist in my family, but not anymore. I have come to realize than unless you do a miraculous work in my parents and in my siblings, there will never be peace. This truth grieves me deeply, and yet I feel your peace within my heart. Please continue to give me the strength and grace to love and serve my parents. You alone can give me the wisdom I need to handle any future disputes or upsets. I know that as long as I seek you first and seek to love them with a pure heart, you will faithfully be at my side, upholding me all the way. Heaven is my real home, filled with other like-minded souls who are like my real family. Amen.

Closing

As I was writing this book, I found myself often down-hearted and discouraged. After a couple of weeks or so of feeling as if I was fighting an uphill battle to find the right words to fully describe what people were going through in their caregiving experiences, I took a little break, called a couple of good friends, and prayed. The friends I spoke with agreed that being called upon to care for elderly parents or relatives often does feel overwhelming. They concurred that it is *not* an easy matter to make major decisions that will greatly impact the people you love.

My friends also reminded me of something I had been missing: Perhaps one of the most important aspects in the big wide world of caregiving is that most individuals are indeed stepping up to the task and giving it their all, even when they aren't getting any thanks, reward, or recognition. Once I realized how faithfully the majority of middle-aged adults do care for their elderly parents, my perspective changed. I saw the entire aging process as something the Lord has designed with redemption in mind. How many people make amends before they pass away? How many petty grievances are finally laid to rest when a family member becomes seriously ill? How many differences of opinion simply vanish because parents and their adult children finally see everything in light of eternity? Lots and lots and lots. Not always, but many do forgive and ask for forgiveness near the end of life.

Let's be honest: aging is difficult for everyone. Older people lose their independence, physical strength, and mental acuity, and often their emotions lack their former stability. All in all, it is hard to age, suffering a multitude of declines. It's equally hard for their younger family members to watch it happen and feel helpless to lessen the impact of their family member's suffering. But God is there for us. Through it all, in the low times and in the high times, God draws close to give us exactly what we need to cope with that day's specific challenges. He never leaves us on our own to handle life's toughest days. Like every other season of life, the Lord wants us to embrace these challenges with confidence that he will be with us, strengthen us, and enable us. God will give them (and us) the grace to die well in the same measure we know and trust him.

On a personal note, as I read others' stories and recalled my own experiences in caregiving, I realized that right now I'm shaping who I will be in twenty years. If I want to be a gentle, kindhearted, grateful, faith-filled elderly woman, then the choices I make today count. Right now, today, I'm deciding who I will be then. If that isn't a sobering thought, then I don't know what is. Taking an up close and personal look at many elderly men and women, I've seen some who are discontented, some who are trying to make the best of it, and the precious few who keep their eyes on Jesus—and because they do, they are the ones who radiate love, joy, and hope. I want to grow into one of those precious few. How about you?

146

Sources for Quotations

1. Oswald Chambers, *My Utmost for His Highest* (Grand Rapids, MI: Discovery House, 1992), November 11 entry.

2. Anne Graham Lotz, *Just Give Me Jesus* (Nashville: W Publishing Group, 2000), 136–37.

3. Tim Lane and Paul David Tripp, *Relationships: A Mess Worth Making* (Greensboro, NC: New Growth Press, 2006), 63.

4. Edward Welch, *Running Scared: Fear, Worry and the God of Rest* (Greensboro, NC: New Growth Press, 2007), 115.

5. Carolyn Custis James, *When Life and Beliefs Collide* (Grand Rapids, MI: Zondervan, 2001), 138.

6. Jerry Bridges, *Trusting God: Even When Life Hurts* (Colorado Springs: NavPress, 1988), 154.

7. Roy Hession, *The Calvary Road* (Fort Washington, PA: CLC Publications, 2001), 28.

8. Nancy Leigh DeMoss, *Choosing Gratitude: Your Journey to Joy* (Chicago: Moody Publishers, 2009), 53.

9. Paula Rinehart, *Strong Women, Soft Hearts* (Nashville: Thomas Nelson, 2001), 104–05.

10. Richard L. Ganz, *The Secret of Self-Control* (Wheaton, IL: Crossway Books, 1998), 47.

11. Edward Welch, *Depression: A Stubborn Darkness* (Winston-Salem, NC: Punch Books, 2006), 222.

12. Arthur Bennett, *The Valley of Vision* (Carlisle, PA: The Banner of Truth Trust, 2002), 24.

13. Bennett, *The Valley of Vision*, 49.

14. Jay Adams, *How to Overcome Evil* (Phillipsburg, NJ: P & R Publishing, 1977), 28.

15. Paul David Tripp, *War of Words* (Phillipsburg, NJ: P & R Publishing, 2000), 145.

16. Hession, *The Calvary Road*, 25.

17. Randy Alcorn, *90 Days of God's Goodness* (Colorado Springs: Multnomah, 2011), 69.

18. Paul David Tripp, *A Shelter in the Time of Storm* (Wheaton, IL: Crossway, 2009), 76.

19. Tripp, *War of Words*, 188.

20. Alcorn, *90 Days of God's Goodness*, 131.

21. John Macarthur, *Found: God's Peace* (Colorado Springs: David C Cook, 1993), 25.

22. Edward Welch, *When People Are Big and God Is Small* (Phillipsburg, NJ: P & R Publishing, 1997), 19.

23. Alcorn, *90 Days of God's Goodness*, 253.

24. Max Lucado, *Everyday Blessings* (Nashville: Thomas Nelson, 2004), 280.

25. Lucado, *Everyday Blessings*, 58.

26. Alcorn, *90 Days of God's Goodness*, 225.

27. James, *When Life and Beliefs Collide*, 73.

28. Richard Burr, *Praying Your Prodigal Home* (Camp Hill, PA: Christian Publications, 2003), 61.

29. Chambers, *My Utmost for His Highest*, December 31 entry.

30. Alcorn, *90 Days of God's Goodness*, 134.